WOMEN OF THE BIBLE SPEAK OUT

STORIES OF
BETRAYAL, ABUSE, HEALING, AND HOPE

MARLO SCHALESKY

Our Daily Bread
Publishing™

Women of the Bible Speak Out: Stories of Betrayal, Abuse, Healing, and Hope
© 2020 by Marlo Schalesky

The author and publisher are not engaged in providing medical or psychological services, and this book is not intended as a guide to diagnose or treat medical or psychological problems. If you are experiencing physical or psychological abuse, or if you need other expert assistance, please consult with a physician or certified counselor immediately.

Requests for permission to quote from this book should be directed to: Permissions Department, Our Daily Bread Publishing, PO Box 3566, Grand Rapids, MI 49501, or contact us by email at permissionsdept@odb.org.

Interior design by Michael J. Williams

Library of Congress Cataloging-in-Publication Data

Names: Schalesky, Marlo M., 1967- author.
Title: Women of the Bible speak out : stories of betrayal, abuse, healing, and hope / Marlo Schalesky.
Description: Grand Rapids, MI : Our Daily Bread Publishing, 2020. |
   Summary: "A study of the biblical text with a focus on God's responses
   to hurting women and how He offers freedom and wholeness"-- Provided by publisher.
Identifiers: LCCN 2020010272 | ISBN 9781640700109 (paperback)
Subjects: LCSH: Women in the Bible--Biography. | Abused women--Religious
   life. | Christian women--Religious life | Spiritual healing.
Classification: LCC BS575 .S337 2020 | DDC 220.9/2082--dc23
LC record available at https://lccn.loc.gov/2020010272

Printed in the United States of America

21 22 23 24 25 26 27 / 8 7 6 5 4 3 2

To my daughters

CONTENTS

She gave this name to the LORD who spoke to her:
"You are the God who sees me."

Genesis 16:13 (NIV)

FOREWORD

Ever since Adam and Eve tasted the sweetness of the forbidden fruit, exploitation and betrayal ruled the earth. People have traded kindness for selfishness, loving their appetites rather than God's ethic. In that fallen state, all sorts of inhumanity flourished. People hurting people decays our world, and we are left with the question, *Why does God allow others to exploit?*

Amidst this backdrop, we also understand the story of Scripture through both Testaments. It is that of a rescue plan, of God the Father sending his Son to dynamically change our stories, from sin-entrenched to kingdom-minded service empowered by the Holy Spirit. It is in this age that we live.

All should be well, right?

Sadly, no.

People still hurt others. Though humanity has been rescued from the power of sin through the life, death, and resurrection of Jesus, sometimes it feels like we're still living in the time of Israel's judges. "In those days Israel had no king;

all the people did whatever seemed right in their own eyes" (Judges 17:6 NLT).

How do we live in an unjust world populated with those who harm others? How do we find healing after betrayal, abuse, slander, or violation? What does the Scripture teach us about thriving in a world bent on our soul destruction?

I have wrestled with this question. As a sexual abuse survivor, a neglected girl, a preyed on daughter, a child of divorces and parental death, I have experienced the consequences of people doing whatever they felt like doing. For a time, this despair immobilized me. I felt powerless to break free of the chains others had foisted upon me.

When I met Jesus at fifteen, those chains began to crack, then break, then fall away. Through the prayers of others, the kindhearted listening by fellow Christ followers, and a lot of empathy I began the long slog toward health. But honestly? The greatest contributor to my healing journey was the Bible. I found myself in its pages. I unearthed the majesty of God folded in, permeating a beautiful narrative of redemption. I did not find robotic people callously shaking off sin or denying its aftereffects. I discovered flawed humanity, yes, but I also uncovered grit and hope. When I placed myself in the story of Scripture, asking myself what would it have been like to be that particular person (who lived, breathed, had hopes and disappointments just like me), the Bible enlivened before me.

That is precisely what *Women of the Bible Speak Out* provides for us all—a pathway through women's narratives, helping us mine their stories for freedom.

Because each of the women highlighted carries a heavy weight.

Each reflects what happens when sin infects a story.

I fear we categorize folks like Hagar or Esther as caricatures, devoid of humanity, reducing them to lifeless sentences on a page rather than considering the very real truth that they ate breakfast, did chores, hoped for a better future, and prayed to God—much like us. And, like us, they endured brokenness, betrayal, abuse, rejection, domination, and shame. Like us, they wondered when the pain would end, or how they'd endure to the next morning. The beauty of their stories is our beauty as well—all are intersected by the God who sees us.

I am grateful for the skillful storytelling of Marlo Schalesky. She helps us understand these women of the Bible, engendering empathy and discernment. But she doesn't stop with storytelling. She expands each story with biblical teaching and wisdom, and provides a clear pathway toward healing. That is why I'm so grateful you picked up this book because I believe you'll be changed for the better.

Healing will come.

Evil will not win.

Your God loves you.

Rest there, friend.

Mary DeMuth

Author of *We Too: How the Church Can Respond Redemptively to the Sexual Abuse Crisis*

INTRODUCTION

An Invitation to Hope and Healing

Twilight shimmers through my office window. I scroll through my newsfeed. #MeToo. The hashtag is familiar now. These days it doesn't create that lump in my throat. It doesn't cause me to shiver or my heart to beat faster. Not anymore. But I remember when it did. I remember the first time it popped up on my screen, when it meant raising a hand and saying that I've experienced it too. So many of us have. Prejudice, abuse, demeaning treatment, injustice, unwanted sexual advances, sexual pressure, and worse. Often much worse. To me, those two words aren't a political statement; they aren't an attempt to shame men. They are simply a way to define a movement that recognizes how much and how many women have suffered because they are women. And so we say, "Me too."

So simple. Two little words. And a lifetime of meaning, of memory, behind them.

To be honest, I don't like #MeToo. I want a world in which it doesn't exist. I want #NobodyAtAll. But that's not the world we live in. This world is far too full of sin, abuse, violence, marginalization, derision, pain, and shame.

I know because I've had my moments too, and while what I really want is to bury them, pretend I live in a world where women are always treated with respect, the #MeToo movement forces me to face the memories and realities that rise up to rattle me, and then still find hope, still see beauty. Still discover the wonder of God in the life I live and the world I live in.

Because one thing I know: God doesn't tolerate pretend. What's hidden in darkness he insists on bringing to the light.

That's just what he did for me one Sunday morning as I stood in church listening to worship music, trying to sing along. Three more #MeToo stories had popped up in my newsfeed that morning. And as I stood, struggling with the disturbance in my soul, God peeled back the layers of memory and I saw again, as if they were new, the moments in my life that I never wanted to remember.

I sat down. Fast.

Though the music continued, I didn't hear it anymore. Instead, I heard the sound of a man's breath when he came into my room where he didn't belong. And though the seat beneath me was soft, I didn't feel it anymore. I felt the rough surface of the wall behind me as I was pushed into it against my will. And I didn't see the lights illuminating the worship team on the platform; instead, I saw opportunities lost because I'm a woman, my words and experience disregarded due to my gender. I saw too much. Heard too much. Felt too much.

Afterward, I spoke to a church friend, mentioning the memories that had haunted me during the service. I expected compassion. I received condemnation. Why hadn't I spoken of this before? Why hadn't I gotten counseling? Why hadn't I done . . . whatever it was I was supposed to do? Why hadn't *I*?

I stood there shaking, broken, not knowing where to turn or what to do. Slowly, I backed away, ran away. Alone, I cried and shuddered and wondered how God would put these broken pieces back together when all I felt was pain.

I still wonder.

What now?

The months have passed. Now I see the posts about an evangelical leader accused of gross misconduct. I see news reports of another stepping down amid substantiated claims of abuse. I see the church flailing, struggling with how to respond to famed leaders who are fallen and the women who have been disbelieved, marginalized, and pushed aside.

And while I'm glad the truth is finally coming to light, sin is being exposed, and justice is coming slowly but steadily, I realize it's not enough.

It's not enough for me.

I want more than justice; I want healing.

I want more than healing; I want wholeness.

I want more than wholeness; I want holiness.

I want God to redeem every bit of my #MeToo experiences, and yours. I want him to transform them all.

I won't be swept up in anger, bitterness, resentment and so be victimized all over again. I won't be battered with the need to assign blame. Healing is not found in the arms of accusation. It's found in a God who sees, loves, and redeems.

I want the wonder of God in the darkest places of life. I want to look at #MeToo and see, in the places I least expect it, the glory of God.

I want resurrection.

Impossible?

I don't think so. Not anymore.

Because I've seen a glimpse of God's wonder in the midst of #MeToo. I believe I know where to find the hope I am looking for. I'm not the first to experience gender-based harassment, marginalization, abuse, and violence. Our generation is not the first to live in this brokenness. Women have come before us, and they have survived. They have thrived. They have overcome and discovered a surprising hope, an unexpected healing, even in the gross inequalities of life. They have encountered God.

What if they could speak to us now? What if they could join their voices to ours? What if they could open the doors and lead the way to a new, deeper understanding of a God who goes far beyond justice to glory?

Through the witness of the women of the Bible—through the grace and glory of God as seen through their eyes—there is a way to healing, wholeness, freedom. New life.

Because God is not sexist. Not now, not ever.

Perhaps, if we walk for a moment in the shoes of Hagar, of Tamar, of Abigail, of a Samaritan woman by a well, we will find new hope, new insight, new healing, new wonder.

In the chapters that follow, we'll listen to these women as they speak out about what happened to them and what they discovered about God through it. As we attend to their stories, our question is not so much, "Who is the bad guy?" though there certainly are some of those. Instead, our primary question is, "Who is God when we find ourselves in these dark places of betrayal, abuse, fear, domination, and despair?" We'll consider what it might have been like for these women in their own #MeToo moments, and how their stories may relate to our own.

The women's stories are presented as first-person, fictional retellings. I've used an approach called *biblical imagination* to fill in unnoted but likely details, to create a sense of culture and setting, and to suggest the emotions and struggles each woman may have experienced. In this sense, the stories build on the factual, but they also reimagine the women in ways that make them relevant to contemporary issues, culture, and questions. Like many of us until recent days, they may not have been able to articulate their objection to the way they were being treated—may not have even noted them as the abuse that they were—but that doesn't make their experiences any less real, any less painful, any less a result of our fallen world. As you read, I hope you will imagine yourself walking with each woman and hearing her story for the first time, or envision yourself sitting with her in a contemporary context, perhaps over a cup of coffee in the intimacy of your own home.

My prayer is that through their stories we will become more than conquerors through him who loves us. For neither death nor life, pain nor shame, disgrace nor degradation, present or future, or any human power is able to separate us from the God who loves us and has called us to be everything he created us to be.

Take a deep breath, straighten your shoulders, and prepare to discover healing, wholeness, and holiness. In those places of deepest hurt, of deepest pain, there is hope that only the wonder of God in the darkest places of life can illuminate. And that hope in God's love for you can heal the deepest wounds.

If you have buried your pain, if you have feared that God may look too much like your abuser, if you are afraid you can never be healed, I invite you to come and walk with me through the lives of these women of old. Come, and for a moment, suspend your fear, quell your doubt. Discover who God is, and who he's always been. Discover this God who invites you to a new hope, a deeper healing, and greater confidence in the woman he created you to be.

Come, walk with me, with these women of the Bible, and with the God who sees you, knows you, and loves you enough to heal the broken places within you.

Marlo

1

EVE

Witness to Brokenness

Genesis 1–3

Adam and his wife were both naked, and they felt no shame. (Genesis 2:25 NIV)

We are all broken. Hurt. Damaged. We are not who we were supposed to be, who God envisioned us to be when he created us. Sin has come into this world and shattered the way we were supposed to be, the way the whole world was created to be. Sin broke our relationship with our Creator, fractured all our relationships. So we live in brokenness—but not in hopelessness.

- - - • • • - - -

It never should have been this way. All the ugliness, all the sorrow and hurt and horror. All the crude comments and lewd actions. Disparaging situations. Demeaning encounters. It was supposed to be so different. It was supposed to be *very good*.

Yet all we get is a glimpse. A brief peek into a world that was breathtaking in its beauty. In its equality. Men, women. Equal in value, status, and significance in creation. Breathtaking in its perfection in which every creature, every blade of grass, every action, every relationship, reflected the wonder of God and the splendor of his love.

The way it was supposed to be.

The way it isn't. Not anymore.

I almost tremble as I look again at the beginning, at the first chapters of Genesis. Because this time I will have to look deeply. Far past the cartoon drawings of a man and woman dressed in splotches of green. Past a shining red apple, a slithering snake, and strategically placed bushes and fig leaves. I will have to confront the magnificence of what should have been. And isn't.

What will I do with that glimpse? What will the first woman whisper to me, to us, through all the millennia that have come between us? How will she speak to us through her own experience, the one that started it all?

What could she say to help us make sense of our own painful relationships?

It could have happened something like this . . .

EVE SPEAKS OUT

I was there when everything was perfect. I opened my eyes for the first time to a blue sky, green trees, kind animals, and a man who loved me, respected me, treated me as equal. I was equal, in every way. Not the same, but equal.

I was there when God sat back and called us very good. Both of us, together. And we were.

I was there when God rested. I was there when the man and I worked the garden together, when we walked with God in the cool of the day. There was no indignity then, no pain, no betrayal or abuse. There was just companionship with our Creator and with each other. The man and I had purpose, together. We worked together, rested together, played together, and strolled the garden with our God together.

And it was good. So very, very good.

Just as it was always supposed to be. The way God created it.

I was there.

I was also there when it was all broken, destroyed.

I wanted knowledge. What I got was pain.

"Did God really say . . . ?" the serpent whispered. So I doubted, I desired, and I ate. The man ate too. And that was the end of the way it was supposed to be.

After we'd eaten the forbidden fruit, we hid in the shadows, ashamed. Ashamed of the bodies we'd once enjoyed. Ashamed of ourselves and each other.

God came to us. And we hid even deeper. We've been hiding ever since. Separately, no longer together.

I crouched there in the trees and listened to the footsteps of my God, walking in the cool of the day just as we had always walked.

"Where are you?" he called.

I didn't answer. The man did. "I heard you in the garden, and I was afraid because I was naked; so I hid."

Naked. We'd always been naked. But now I was embarrassed by it, and so was he. Now it was vulnerability. Now it was shame. I had never felt this way before. Now it became the only thing I knew. The only thing I could feel.

Shame.

The Creator drew closer, his face aglow with the same love he'd always shown, and something else. As if the love caused him . . . pain? Pain, that was new to me too.

"Who told you that you were naked? Have you eaten from the tree that I commanded you not to eat from?"

Yes. The answer was so simple. Yet I couldn't speak it. The man didn't speak it either. We never spoke it. Either of us. Instead, two words came from the man's mouth, two words that shattered our relationship.

"The woman . . ."

He pointed at me. He blamed me.

"The woman you put here with me—she gave me some fruit from the tree, and I ate it."

Those words heralded the brokenness of relationship that our sin had caused.

The woman did it.

The equality, the partnership, the trust, the love on which our very lives had been built, crumbled. It was broken by our sin and proclaimed by two words: *The woman . . .*

With sin came blame and hate, fear and abuse.

He used me to deflect his guilt.

It was never supposed to be that way.

Then the Lord God turned to me. "What is this you have done?"

I sinned. The answer was so simple. But I couldn't speak it either. The man thought blaming me would free him. Instead, it only broke us further. So why did I think I could somehow free myself by blaming another? I don't know. And yet, I pointed to the snake. "The serpent deceived me, and I ate."

God turned and cursed the serpent. He put it under the feet of my offspring. Then he turned to me. Would he put me under the feet of the man? Would he place me beneath as he did the serpent?

He did not. He didn't even curse me. Instead, he spoke of consequences. Pain in childbirth, and something I shiver now to understand. "Your desire will be for your husband, and he will rule over you."

Rule over me. This was not the way it was supposed to be. This conflict, this shame. This tension between desire and command. Between the need to be together and the need to control. We were not created this way. God did not choose it. He made us of equal value, not one above the other, one more important than the other, one more esteemed, honored, respected, significant. He made us two people who *together* reflected his glory, all the glory of creation. We were very good.

And now we were not.

He made us clothes and banished us from the garden. Cherubim swooped from the sky to bar the way back with a flaming, flashing sword.

He looked at me as we left him, and I knew, I knew with all the knowledge of good and evil I had gained, that this God was good. He would not allow us to eat from the tree of life and so condemn us to this broken state forever. He would redeem us. He would make a way back to the beauty we'd left behind, to right relationship, to peace.

Somehow, the brokenness between us would be redeemed. Somehow. But for now, I live in the consequences of a world, of a relationship, marred by sin.

And I must learn to find God, to find good again, in it.

I must believe that this is not the end. It is only a broken beginning.

Witness to Brokenness

It's so difficult to begin. So difficult to look at this deep divide between men and women and the pain that has come from it. I want to look away. I want to believe it's really not that bad. But I know better. And so do you.

The world God created, the humans he made to inhabit it, were always supposed to be equal in value, united, strong, innocent, free. They were supposed to be the very epitome of God's image in creation.

It was a beautiful plan. A beautiful reality. And all too brief.

A Beautiful Equality

We were meant for equality. The truth of it is plain from the first chapter of the Scriptures:

> So God created human beings in his own image. In the image of God he created them; male and female he created them. Then God blessed them and said, "Be fruitful and multiply. Fill the earth and govern it. Reign over the fish in the sea, the birds in the sky, and all the animals that scurry along the ground." (Genesis 1:27–28 NLT)

He created us male and female, equally. He blessed us equally. He gave us dominion over the fish, birds, and every living creature, equally. His was an equal call to care for creation, to live in his image, and to be blessed. Equal. Not the same. Not identical. But not one lesser and one greater either.

In Genesis 2:18, we read God's words: "It is not good for the man to be alone. I will make a helper suitable for him" (NIV). The way some interpret that passage is as though God created women for the sole purpose of serving men. But reading this as a hierarchical structure does not do justice to the fullness and beauty of God's creative intentions as seen in the original language.

In Hebrew, the words translated "helper suitable" are *ezer kenegdo*. *Ezer*, or "helper," is actually a masculine noun the biblical writers also used of God:

- "Hear, LORD, the cry of Judah . . . . Oh, be his help [*ezer*] against his foes!" (Deuteronomy 33:7 NIV)
- "LORD, be my help [*ezer*]" (Psalm 30:10 NIV).
- "Surely God is my help [*ezer*]" (Psalm 54:4 NIV).
- "You are destroyed, Israel, because you are against me, against your helper [*ezer*]" (Hosea 13:9 NIV).

Surely God is not *lesser*. God as our *ezer* is not to be ruled and dominated by a human being, male or female. So we need to look deeper to understand what it means that Eve was an *ezer kenegdo*.

The root of the Hebrew word *ezer* connotes strength or power. *Kenegdo*, the word translated "suitable," has the connotations of being appropriate for the situation, being right, corresponding to. When we look at the two Hebrew words together, *ezer kenegdo*—a helper/power/strength that is suitable/corresponding to—we again see this idea that man and woman, equal in power, were to care for each other and to care for creation together. "Suitable helper" was never meant to indicate a hierarchy in which women were subordinate to men. It was intended as a beautiful partnership of corresponding strength that would reflect the very heart of God and his love for his creation. Together, as corresponding powers, men and women were created with strength to be all God had purposed (Genesis 2:18). And that was *very good*.

Genesis goes on to affirm that man and woman were made for each other and were intended to work together as one, united in relationship to God and the world around them. Adam said of Eve, "This is now bone of my bones and flesh of my flesh; she shall be called 'woman,' for she was taken out of man" (Genesis 2:23 NIV). The biblical writer then adds, "That is why a man leaves his father and mother and is united to his wife, and they become one flesh" (Genesis 2:24 NIV). One flesh. Not one taking advantage of the other. But just as the law and Jesus commands us to, "Love your neighbor as yourself" (Leviticus 19:18; Matthew 22:39; Romans 13:9), men and women were to be united, caring for each other, strengthening each other, walking together with their God.

The Genesis text goes on to say, "Adam and his wife were both naked, and they felt no shame" (Genesis 2:25 NIV). No shame. Not for the woman, not for the man. Sexuality was never supposed to be something that was used to dominate, abuse, shame, or subdue. It was supposed to be something to celebrate and rejoice in, equally. They were *both* naked. And there was no shame.

What a beautiful picture of what God intended, how he created, how man and woman together would reflect the image of God!

And Then . . .

But it didn't last. Instead, sin made sexuality shameful. As soon as Adam and Eve ate the forbidden fruit, they became ashamed of their bodies and sewed together fig leaves to cover themselves (Genesis 3:7). Shame entered the relationship between man and woman.

God then walked in the garden and called to them. But they were hidden. For the first time, hiddenness, pretense, and deception entered their relationship with God. They pretended they weren't there. They tried to trick God into leaving them alone.

We do the same. We hide, we sew fig leaves, we pretend what happened didn't happen at all. But just as in Genesis,

God is calling men and women out of their hiding to face the truth together with him. Only then can we move through justice into healing.

Ever since Adam and Eve, men and women have tried to hide the truth from God and others. But as Paul says in his first letter to the church at Corinth, God "will bring to light what is hidden in darkness and will expose the motives of the heart" (1 Corinthians 4:5 NIV). God calls us out of hiding and into the light of his truth. Into an encounter with the God who loves men and women equally.

But fear often stops us from approaching God. "I heard you in the garden," said the man, "and I was afraid because I was naked; so I hid" (Genesis 3:10 NIV). Fear of what others— in this case, God—will think. Fear of consequences. Fear of being found out and exposed. But fear never leads to healing. We must come out of the bushes, even trembling, to our God.

In addition, when fear entered the relationship between God, man, and woman, blame entered with it. When questioned by God, the man immediately hid in a new way—he hid behind a finger pointed at the woman. "The woman you put here with me . . . ," he said. No longer were the man and woman one. Instead, they were divided, opposing entities, each trying to shift blame. The man shifted blame to the woman. The woman shifted blame to the snake. So—along with shame—pretense, fear, and blame became a significant part of the relationship between the sexes.

And so it has been ever since. Abuse, degradation, marginalization, every gender-humiliating moment you can imagine, are all reflections of that brokenness between the first man and first woman, of Adam shifting his own guilt, grief, stress, pain, fear, shame, and blame onto Eve.

But God never says to Adam, "Oh, it's Eve's fault. I guess you're off the hook." And he doesn't say that to men today.

Attempts to justify abuse because a woman dressed a certain way, spoke a certain way, walked a certain way, glanced a certain way, is just as wrong now as it was then. Then, as now, God doesn't accept any form of "the woman made me do it" as justification for sin.

With God, blame isn't important. It doesn't matter if it's the man's fault, the woman's fault, the snake's fault. Consequences come all the same.

Consequences

Contrary to popular thought, just two things are cursed by God in Genesis 3: the serpent in verse 14 and the ground in verse 17. Not the woman. Not the man. What they experience is not *curses* but *consequences*. And in the midst of those consequences, God layers in hope.

The man will sweat, but he will eat.

The woman will be in pain, but she will bear children.

Life will be hard, but they will live.

The same dichotomy has also colored the relationship between men and women ever since. Relationship will be difficult, but it can also bring life.

Significantly, while God places the serpent under the feet of the woman's offspring, he does not place the woman under the feet of man. Instead, it is only together—through their offspring—that the serpent will be vanquished. Even in their broken condition, caused by sin, God did not create a hierarchy, but called for an equality and unity to crush the serpent's head. This does not mean that every woman must have a man to be complete, nor every man have a woman. But in general, victory requires the sexes working together, in a reflection of God's original plan of unity.

Inequality is not a curse, it is a consequence of sin. The implications of God's pronouncement make it clear: "Your desire will be for your husband, and he will rule over you" (Genesis 3:16 NIV). God declares here the consequences of sin that women have experienced ever since. God does not *ordain* the consequence, but simply acknowledges it. Because of sin, the equality created from the very beginning is broken and replaced by the desire for dominance. It was never supposed to be this way.

God created men and women as equally significant. They were to be corresponding powers to care for and govern creation together. Male dominance, and the abuse, degradation, mistreatment, and exploitation that often come with it, is an unhappy consequence of sin and brokenness. God never ordained or condoned it. And he doesn't condone it now.

Through the rest of the biblical story (as we will see in the following chapters), God works to restore both women and men to "the way it was supposed to be," to a right relationship between the sexes, and with himself. He works to redeem what was broken.

Who Is God in Our Brokenness?

What does God say to us through the story of Eve? The God who forbade eating from the tree of the knowledge of good and evil, who walked the garden, who called the man and the woman out of hiding? The One who promised the crushing of the serpent's head?

Even now, it breaks my heart, my soul, to ponder deeply all that was lost through sin, and the breathtaking beauty that was shattered in that single act of defiance in Genesis 3. And even now, I am surprised when I hear yet another story of abuse and betrayal. I am always surprised. I am always appalled. I will never get used to the destructive horrors of sin. While I know this is the world we live in, I also know with every fiber of my being that this is just not right. It's not the way it was meant to be. Blame and shame, use and abuse, have no rightful place in the world as it was created. There is no excuse. There is no reasoning. It is simply wrong. And in my very being, I revolt against the wrongness.

But then I look deeper. And I wonder if, through the very pain and shame, a new sense of courage might be found, a strong whisper of a hope I never dreamed of. I need that hope. In the brokenness that has come down me, to us, through the millennia, I want to find the grace and glory God wove into time from the very beginning. I want to see as Eve saw, and perhaps renew my vision of this damaged world.

Because despite the consequences of sin, God whispers a redeeming vision. And it happened when he banished Adam and Eve from the garden. "He must not be allowed to reach out his hand and take also from the tree of life and eat, and live forever," God says in Genesis 3:22 (NIV).

It seems like another unhappy consequence. And it would be except for God's reason: *So they won't live forever.* In other words, banishment is a *mercy.* God does not want human beings to live forever in a corrupted and broken state. It is a mercy that means we won't live with pain and abuse forever. We won't be stuck with blame, shame, sin, degradation, fear, and every other thing that invaded our lives with the entrance of sin.

And that's why there's hope.

God barred the way back to the garden because he intended, he always intended, to redeem it all. The rest of the Bible, the rest of human history, is focused on this one thing—recreating what was destroyed. And that includes the relationship between men and women.

So, what would Eve say to us? What might we hear from this woman who was there when everything was as it should be, and who was there when it became what it is? I think she would say to us, "Have hope!" The God who walked in the garden, who created everything, even man and woman, and called it "very good," has never let go of his intention for unity, equality, and glory. His dream of a beautiful creation the way it was meant to be is not lost. He will never settle for the brokenness of Genesis 3. He hasn't given up. On creation. Or on you. He never will.

No matter the severity of the injustice that has happened to you, or to me, no matter the pain and the shame, no matter how long the wrongness has lasted, we can't give up. We continue to hope. We continue to dream. We continue to work toward a world in which we propagate God's will—of man and woman equally, together, reflecting the wonder and glory of our Creator who loves us.

The days may seem dark, the work difficult, the way to the garden forever barred. But God is creating another way. He has never stopped working toward our redemption. And nothing sin has caused is beyond the reach of the One who created us the way we were supposed to be.

> I say to you, my friends, that even though we must face the difficulties of today and tomorrow, I still have a dream . . . . I have a dream that one day every valley shall be exalted, every hill and mountain shall be made low, the rough places will be made plain, and the crooked places shall be made straight and the glory of the Lord will be revealed and all flesh shall see it together.
>
> This is our hope.
>
> Martin Luther King Jr.,
> "I Have a Dream"

2

SARAI

Betrayed

Genesis 12, 20

This is how you can show your love to me: Everywhere we go, say of me, "He is my brother." (Genesis 20:13 NIV)

We trust. We believe. We put our hope, our lives, into the hands of another. And sometimes, instead of safety, we find betrayal. We are exposed to hurt, danger, abandonment—mistreated by the very one(s) we trusted to protect us. It isn't right.

——— · · · ———

A woman sits across the table from me. We order coffee. I leave my paper, my pen, in my bag. She doesn't want her story recorded. She'll only tell it once. I wait as she adjusts the jacket of her business suit, smooths hair already pulled back in a bun, places her hands carefully on the wooden tabletop. Her manicured nails gleam. She looks like any other businesswoman having coffee with an associate. Nothing stands out. Nothing to warn me of the story she would tell.

And then she begins.

She tells me of a little girl barely five years old. She tells me of heroin-addicted parents, of living in a box in an alleyway, of beatings and starvation and cold nights when she cried herself to sleep. Then she pauses. Her voice lowers. And she tells me how those parents sold that little girl over and over for nothing more than the next fix.

Her gaze rises to lock with mine, my eyes wet with tears, hers as dry as dirt. "They went to jail," she says. "They got out. But how does that little girl ever get free?"

I close my eyes, unable to meet the question in hers. "I don't know," I whisper. "I don't know."

How do you heal when the very people who are supposed to protect you betray you instead?

As I sat there in the coffee shop grappling with the horrors of one woman's story, I realized that her question belongs to us all. How do we get free, especially when our greatest hurt, the most significant damage done to our souls, comes from those closest to us—from those we trusted, from those we loved and who said they loved us.

What kind of love is that?

And what does faith look like then? What does hope look like?

━━━ • • • ━━━

In the book of Genesis, Sarai, the woman who would later be renamed Sarah, Abraham's wife, experienced that kind of betrayal at the hands of her husband, a man she had trusted and stuck beside as they left the security of Ur to follow God's promises. At least twice (and likely many times more) he denied her the protection of marriage, leaving her vulnerable to sexual violation. At least twice his fears were more important to him than her safety. At least twice he used her to protect himself, and was enriched by placing her in danger.

Typically, when we study Sarah, we focus on her infertility and God's promise of a son. But there are other parts of her story often overlooked. Intimate parts that reveal a woman betrayed, a woman who may understand and relate to our own painful betrayals by those closest to us. She can help us find hope when love isn't love at all.

For Sarai, it may have happened like this . . .

SARAI SPEAKS OUT

I trusted him. When he said the Lord had spoken and we must abandon the comforts of Ur, I followed him. When we were stuck in Haran, halfway between the land of promise and the place of the past, I waited with him. When we left for Canaan, I walked at his side. I helped him pitch our tents by the great oaks in Shechem. I settled with him as a foreigner in a land promised to us by our God.

And then we left it. Famine came. He chose to go to Egypt. And I followed. I trusted. Of course I did.

When we arrived in the land of Pharaoh, Abram was afraid. He was not wise, he was not kind, when he was afraid.

And that's when he turned to me, that eve as we crossed the border of Egypt and left the promises behind. "I know what a beautiful woman you are," he said. It wasn't a compliment. "When the

Egyptians see you, they will say, 'This is his wife.' Then they will kill me but will let you live."

Live, yes. But, oh, didn't he know what it would mean for me? "Say you are my sister," he said, "so that I will be treated well for your sake and my life will be spared because of you."

So *his* life would be better. So *he* would be spared. Didn't he know that as a sister, I could be bought by anyone? Taken? Abused? Yes, he knew. But he didn't care. He didn't even consider it.

At that moment, I became no more than a pawn. A shield. A possession to be bartered. I was not a wife.

I was exposed. Betrayed.

He may as well have led me through the streets, his rope around my neck, calling out, "Fine cow for slaughter!" I am not a cow. I am a woman. A married woman. Marriage was supposed to be a protection for me. But he stole that from me and made me agree to the deception.

He said it himself: They would have let me live.

But he had no concern for me. He cared only about his own safety, his own life, his own wealth and well-being.

What about me? Did anyone care about me?

Sure enough, I was sold, brought to the harems of Pharaoh. And there was nothing I could do to save myself, to protect myself.

I sat in the dimness of the harem's walls, waiting for Pharaoh to call me, to violate me. I could do nothing but wait. I had no power there.

I waited. I worried. I sat and shivered and prayed and wondered. I lived in fear while my husband-turned-brother, I later learned, was honored with sheep, oxen, donkeys, servants, and camels. He had everything. I had nothing. Less than nothing.

In the Lord's great mercy, the call to the Pharaoh's bedchamber never came. Instead, one day a eunuch led me to the throne room. Pharaoh sat above, with my so-called brother standing below him.

I didn't know why he was there. I didn't know why I was there. But there were rumors. Rumors of great plagues afflicting the house of Pharaoh because of me, because I was Abram's wife.

I will never forget Pharaoh's words to my husband. They ring in my ears still. "What is this you have done to me?" he declared. "Why did you not tell me that she was your wife?" His finger stabbed toward me. "Why did you say, 'She is my sister,' so that I took her for my wife? Now then, here is your wife; take her, and go."

His servants hurried us from the palace. And Abram hurried us away from Egypt, with more donkeys and oxen, slaves, and an Egyptian maidservant for me.

Abram chose a lie. I could not oppose it. But God could. He did. The truth set me free. It set Abram free too.

You would think he'd have learned.

But he didn't. Everywhere we went, he insisted I say he was my brother. He said to me, "This is the kindness you must do me: at every place to which we come, say of me, 'He is my brother.'" At every place! I wasn't safe anywhere. The harems of Pharaoh were not the end. They were only the beginning.

A kindness, he called it. Kindness? Is it kind to demand that if I really loved him, I would sacrifice myself to this lie?

I did it. But a lie is never love.

Years passed, and we came to the land of Gerar, where Abimelech was king. God had changed our names by then. I was no longer Sarai, but Sarah. And Abram had become Abraham, father of many. He held the promise in his very name. We would have a son. Through us would come nations, and descendants as innumerable as the stars.

And yet, he was still afraid of being killed because of me. What kind of faith is that? Would God really allow anyone to kill him after the promise was made? After God called us from Ur, rescued me from famine and Pharaoh, and gave us new names?

But Abraham didn't think of that. He didn't trust in our God, and so I was taken again. Taken by Abimelech, another king.

This time, the Lord made the king's household infertile. Oh, the irony! Abraham gave away the one with whom he was supposed to have a child, and the consequence was that no others could conceive. Even this foreign ruler knew it was wrong. He had more faith than a man whose name held the promise of a covenant with God Almighty.

So Abraham was dragged before a king again, reprimanded again, and given sheep and oxen and servants. Again.

But instead of simply sending us away, the king turned to me. He spoke to me, and his words were like the very words of my God. "Behold, I have given your brother a thousand pieces of silver," he said. "It is a sign of your innocence in the eyes of all who are with you, and before everyone you are vindicated."

Vindicated! At last! Everything was finally set right.

Not by my husband, but by God himself, through this king.

My husband betrayed me. He put me in danger for his own safety, his own gain. But God was my advocate. He was my savior. He was more husband to me than Abraham ever could be. And in the end, he made all things right. Even in the harem of Pharaoh, even in the house of Abimelech, I was never alone.

And so, I can survive. I can thrive. Because there is One who loves me enough to set me free from every lie.

Betrayed

Love protects, trusts, hopes, perseveres (1 Corinthians 13:7). It does not use, abuse, take, and steal. It does not lie. It does not betray the beloved. But sometimes those who are supposed to love us, do not. Parents, husbands, brothers, uncles, neighbors, coaches, friends. Sometimes, like Sarah, we are betrayed. For Sarah, that betrayal came in the form of a husband who put her in a position to be taken by other men.

First, Abram chose to go to Egypt, out of the land promised to him by God. The fear of want drove him. A famine had come. He was unsure that he would get all he needed. Sarai had no choice but to follow.

As they entered Egypt, Abram became afraid that he'd be killed by men who wanted his wife, even though the killing of a husband to attain a wife does not seem to have been a common practice in ancient Egypt. In fact, outside of the biblical account of Abram's fears, there is no documentation of such a practice. Egyptian scholars agree that ancient Egyptians were monogamous. Typically, only Pharaoh had multiple wives in addition to the primary wife, called the Great Royal Wife. Nevertheless, the fear of harm drove Abram to a lie. He forced Sarai to put herself in the compromised position of sister. While she was technically his half-sister (daughter of his father but not his mother, as explained in Genesis 20), her relationship with Abram was most definitely that of wife. But as his sister, she was essentially up for grabs, up for sale to the highest bidder.

And he blamed her for it: *It's because you're a beautiful woman*, he says (Genesis 12:11). It's her fault because she's so beautiful. Sound familiar?

Abram's betrayal runs deep. He not only removed the protection of her status as his wife, but he also made her responsible—for his fears and his lies.

When Love Isn't Love

"This is how you can show your love to me," Abraham says, "Everywhere we go, say of me, 'He is my brother'" (Genesis 20:13 NIV). In other words, "If you really love me, you will . . ." *You will do what I say, you will protect me, you will agree to what's bad for you just because I want it.* Some manipulations have been around for millennia.

And it's time for women to stop giving in to the lie. Nothing is our fault because we're too beautiful. It's not our place to accept abuse in the name of love.

Such love isn't love at all.

When love is used as an excuse for bad behavior, that is a betrayal. A betrayal of the loved one, a betrayal of the very nature of love, and a betrayal of God himself, who is love—the real thing.

Abraham betrayed Sarah when he removed the protection of marriage and cast her into a dangerous, sexually vulnerable position. He betrayed love by thinking only of his safety and well-being while simultaneously sacrificing hers. He betrayed God by failing to honor the woman God had given him for a wife and co-covenant holder.

And there was little Sarah could do about it. In her day, women did not have the voice they do today. They could be taken, bartered, sold, acquired as possessions. Genesis 12 and 20 both emphasize Sarah's helplessness by never giving her a voice in the text itself. In neither story does she utter a single word. The biblical text does show her speaking in other passages, but in these two, she is very present and very silent. Yet, she did have power over one thing—she didn't have to believe the lie of "If you really loved me . . ." Real love does not express itself in faithlessness, manipulation, lies, or betrayal.

Even though she went along with her husband's lie, God did not. He never does. That much is clear in the text.

Abraham was her husband, and he had no right to use her to assuage his own fears. In both incidents, God rebukes Abraham through the words of foreign kings. Pharaoh says to him, "What is this you have done to me? Why did you not tell me that she was your wife?" (Genesis 12:18). Abimelech's rebuke is stronger yet: "What have you done to us? And how have I sinned against you, that you have brought on me and my kingdom a great sin? You have done to me things that ought not to be done" (Genesis 20:9).

What Abraham did ought not be done. Even heathen kings knew it. Abraham failed. His faith failed. His trust in God failed. His love failed. It failed God, and it failed his co-recipient of God's sacred promises.

In Genesis 17, when Abram received his new name, Abraham, Sarah also was renamed as part of the covenant promise. Old Testament scholar Gordon Wenham remarks, "At this point, one might have anticipated that the Lord would have stopped speaking [after renaming Abram]. Both sides of the covenant have been explained. . . . But instead God goes on talking . . . announc[ing] that Sarai's name must be changed to Sarah."[1]

Like Sarah, women are equal partners in all the promises of God. When women are treated as less than, as possessions, as something to be used to bolster a man's status, confidence, or security, God's purposes are thwarted. That isn't love.

Sometimes this betrayal is as severe as that experienced by my friend whose parents traded her for drugs. Sometimes, however, the betrayal is more subtle. A couple of my daughters are to the age where they are dating, so we've been talking about the difference between real love and self-centered "love." It seems easy for young men to proclaim, "I'm so in love with you," but much harder to demonstrate the behavior that supports their declarations. To many, it seems love is not about doing what's best for the other, but rather about a warm, fuzzy feeling in the person making the declaration. Usually, such "love" focuses on how you make *me* feel about *me*. That isn't love.

Self-centered love is one-sided. It takes. Real love is mutual. It both gives and receives.

Self-centered love makes the other person into an idol, the one who is supposed to fulfill all wants and needs and assuage all fears. But real love invites couples to trust God together, look to him together, follow him together.

Self-centered love demands attention, but real love seeks not attention but what is mutually beneficial to all.

Self-centered love is exactly the type of love Abraham demonstrated. He required Sarah to sacrifice her safety so he could feel safe, sacrifice her own well-being so he could gain status—donkeys, servants, cattle, and other measures of wealth. This is not love. It's betrayal. It's abuse.

"If you love me, you will . . ." Not love. Abuse.

"You can't leave me, what would I do without you?" Not love. Abuse.

"I'm just trying to show my love [with unwanted physical advances]." Not love. Abuse.

"Why won't you let me . . ." Not love. Abuse.

"I'll be hurt if you don't . . ." Not love. Abuse.

The list could go on and on and on. So what do we do? What does real love look like?

When Love Is Love

Sarah's story demonstrates at least four truths about love, four ways we can know when love is really love. To understand real love in Sarah's story, and our own, we look not to Abraham but to God. Whereas Abraham considered his wife less valuable than himself, God did not. He did not approve or tolerate this treatment. To God, Sarah was precious. And so are you. Here are some things we can learn about real love from God's interaction with Sarah.

Love knows who you really are. "But the LORD afflicted Pharaoh and his house with great plagues because of *Sarai, Abram's wife*" (Genesis 12:17, emphasis added). No one else in the story uses her name. Abram calls her sister (verse 13). The Egyptians call her "the woman" (verses 14 and 15). But when God is involved, Sarai has a name, and the proper rank of wife. God knows who she really is. He never resorts to lies. And, as mentioned above, when it came time to rename Abram, Sarai received a new name from God as well. God says, "As for Sarai your wife, you shall not call her name Sarai, but Sarah shall be her name. I will bless her, and moreover, I will give you a son by her. I will bless her, and she shall become nations; kings of peoples shall come from her" (Genesis 17:15–16).

Twice, the same number of times kings would claim her because of a lie, God links her name to blessing. Twice, he ties her new name to the covenant promises. And in doing so, he redeems what happened with Pharaoh in her past and what will happen with Abimelech in her future. In addition, by naming her, God claims her for himself. The act of bestowing a name is a sign of authority and of intimacy. Parents name their children. God named her Sarah, which means "my princess." She was his. Abraham may have betrayed her by not claiming her as wife, but God, in his love, claimed her as his own precious princess and called her by her true name and her true position. With God, there were no lies.

God knows who you are, too. He calls you by name. You are not what others may claim. You are valued. You are precious. You can be a co-recipient of the glorious promises and blessings of God. You are beloved. And you can be his.

Love calls wrong, wrong. It calls evil, evil. It makes no excuses. It tells no lies. Both times Sarah was claimed by kings, God prompted those kings to tell the truth about the wickedness of what Abraham had done. There is no doubt from Pharaoh's words in Genesis 12:18 that the claim of "she is my sister" was an unconscionable offense. Abimelech, whom God warned in a dream, expressed the even stronger reprimand when he accused Abraham of bringing a great sin on him and his kingdom, and boldly declared that what Abraham did was wrong (Genesis 20:9). Abraham then made excuses, tried to soften his sin by claiming Sarah was his sister, a half-sister. But neither God nor Abimelech accepted the excuse. Never in the whole of the Bible does God call Sarah Abraham's sister. She is always his wife. In Sarah's life, and in our own, God never softens the wrongness of sin. He never justifies it. He never downplays it. He doesn't even look the other way. Love never makes excuses for sin.

Love gives a voice to the voiceless. As mentioned, Sarah was completely silent in both Genesis 12 and 20, which was not unusual for women in the cultures of that day. But God prompted both Pharaoh and Abimelech to speak for her. "What have you done to me?" they both say—the very words Sarah cannot speak for herself. "You have done things that ought not be done!" Abimelech asserts. Through these men, God gave Sarah a voice even when others, even when the culture, did not. And it was the voice of kings!

Love redeems. In both stories, Sarah was rescued and restored to her proper position. In the second, she was also exonerated, set free from any wrongdoing. King Abimelech said to her directly, "Behold, I have given your brother a thousand pieces of silver. It is a sign of your innocence in the eyes of all who are with you, and before everyone you are vindicated" (Genesis 20:16). The New International Version puts it this way: "I am giving your brother a thousand shekels of silver. This is to cover the offense against you before all who are with you; you are completely vindicated." *Vindicated*, justified, defended, proven correct, not to blame, on the right side—even without Abraham claiming his proper role as husband. Abimelech still called him "your brother," and yet his kingly declaration redeemed all the years of betrayal, all the times she had to say, "He is my brother" and participate in a lie that put her in jeopardy. Before Abraham intervened, while he was still caught in the lie, Sarah was set free, and never again do we hear about Abraham pressuring her into this lie and betraying her in this way.

The most powerful person in the land, the king, declared Sarah's righteousness. The most powerful person ever, the King Jesus, has the authority to declare yours—whether or not the ones who betrayed you have repented of their ways. Whether or not they still cling to their lies. Your king vindicates you, justifies you. You are not to blame for the wrong others have done to you. Love redeems. Love sets free.

Even so, there may be times when it seems as if God is silent, distant, absent, as if rescue came for Sarah but not for you. To you I say, don't give up on God's love. Your story isn't over. Sarah spent long nights in the dark, in the harem of Pharaoh, in the house of Abimelech. She spent years struggling with the fear and damage of a lie. But God saw, he knew, and he had a plan to redeem her. To redeem her fear, her shame, her doubts.

When you are betrayed by someone you trusted, when love isn't love at all, when you are manipulated, hurt, voiceless, know that God sees, God cares, God redeems.

We heal in part by embracing our value to God, by living as much as we possibly can, each day, in the reality that we are *his*. When we accept his kingship, we accept that we are

Sarah—his princess. He claims us as his own, precious to him, and declares that we are free from the lies others tell.

Who Is God When We're Betrayed?

Our God deems us precious. Valuable. Righteous. Justified. Free. *Loved.*

All of that is true. Of you, and of me. And yet, if it's true, why doesn't this God who loves us always save us before anything bad happens? What if the abuse occurs again and again? How could he let us be betrayed and hurt and violated?

Can we trust his love even then?

I don't have all the answers. But I do know that God also didn't spare his only Son.

Jesus trusted his Father in heaven. He loved, he gave, he never sinned . . . and yet he was betrayed. By a kiss, no less! By a sign of love. On the night he was arrested, Judas, one of Jesus's closest friends, one of the twelve special disciples, a man who walked with Jesus, lived with him, and claimed devotion to him, walked up to Jesus in front of a mob of soldiers with torches and swords, and kissed him. The kiss was to show the mob what man to arrest. And following that kiss, Jesus was arrested, beaten, mocked, and crucified. A kiss is a sign of affection, but behind this kiss was the worst kind of betrayal.

Our God, in Christ, has lived the pain of betrayal. For him, it led to a horrific death on a Roman cross. It led to the most excruciating and cruel execution known to the world at that time. He was beaten, mocked, and crucified because he was betrayed by someone who claimed to love him, someone who betrayed him with a kiss.

Many of us have been there too. There were promises of love, kisses, but love wasn't love. It wasn't the real thing. And

Jesus shows us how to respond to that kind of betrayal. As he hung on the cross, his last words were, "Father, into your hands I commit my spirit!" (Luke 23:46). For him, it was a cry of surrendering to death; for us, it can be a daring, courageous cry of surrendering to real love, true love, the love that never abandons, never betrays. The love that knows your name, makes no excuses, gives you the voice of kings, and redeems you. The love that makes you an equal recipient of the promises of God. The love that sets you free from all guilt, all shame, and calls you his own. His princess.

Commit your spirit to him. You can withstand this pain because Jesus has walked this path of betrayal before you, and he walks beside you now. You can flourish. It's not easy. It's never easy. But Jesus himself has shown the way and holds your hand as you travel the path of healing your soul. Because he suffered and died and rose from the grave, you can be fully healed.

In the face of betrayal, stand in the love of Christ. Place your hand, place your life, in his. Hear the words of God spoken over you through Abimelech, the king: *You are innocent . . . and before everyone you are vindicated. You are seen. You are loved. You are valued.*

And no one can take that away.

> Love works in miracles every day: such as weakening the strong, and stretching the weak.
>
> Margaret de Valois (1553–1615)

3

HAGAR
Used

Genesis 16, 21

She called the name of the LORD who spoke
to her, "You are a God of seeing," for she said,
"Truly here I have seen him who looks after me."
(Genesis 16:13)

Used. And tossed aside. Sometimes we are not valued for
who we are but rather for how we can be exploited for
another's advantage. Users take what they want and leave us
with nothing once our usefulness to them has passed. But
God didn't create us to be used and discarded.

* * *

My heart breaks as I hear her story. Her family fled Mexico
when she was a baby. They came to California. As soon as she

was old enough, she picked berries in the fields. She traveled from town to town, tiny fingers picking. Tiny back bending. Tiny legs hurrying up and down rows. Then she hit puberty. Now she could be used for something more than berry picking. So she was. She was given to a man over twice her age so that her parents could gain some economic advantage. The man didn't marry her, he just used her to satisfy his lusts, to get what he wanted. After a few years passed and he had all that he wanted of her, he cast her aside. With nothing. No virginity. No education. No family. No money. No job. No country, even, to call her own. Used, and tossed aside.

As I swallowed the tears gathered in my throat, I thought, *I've heard this story before.* But the girl wasn't from Mexico, she was from Egypt. Her name was Hagar. She, too, was used by others—by Sarai and Abram—to get what they wanted. And when she had exceeded her usefulness, she was left with nothing.

Or at least, that's how it seemed.

But I wonder, if we let Hagar speak, if we listen carefully to the story she tells, will we find a different truth, a different reality for those who have been used and cast aside? Might we find hope and healing for those of us who share a similar story? Might we even find the wonder of God in the heartbreaking story of a young woman in a foreign land who appeared to have lost everything?

HAGAR SPEAKS OUT

It wasn't supposed to be like this. My life was planned. From birth. Like my mother and her mother before her, I was a servant in the house of Pharaoh. An honorable position. A safe one.

But all that changed once Pharaoh took *that* woman as a wife. A foreigner. Beautiful. But deadly.

No one knew she was another man's wife. No one thought a thing of it until the diseases started. No one was left unaffected. The whole of Pharaoh's house was afflicted. Including me, and I was but a child.

That's how we discovered their deception. And we paid the price. Yes, and I paid it more than most. Pharaoh gave the foreign man sheep, oxen, donkeys, camels—and servants. He gave me to that woman.

Then Pharaoh sent us away—away from my family, my home, my country.

Now I was the foreigner. We traveled to Canaan, that backward land of dust and oaks and no Pharaoh. And we settled in tents. Tents! I, who was used to the comforts of Pharaoh's palace, became a tent-dwelling nobody—reduced to the status of handmaiden to a foreign woman who paid me no heed.

If only it would have stayed that way. But it didn't.

Months turned to years and my mistress's waist stayed slim. I would hear her sometimes, muttering, praying to her foreign god. Did he listen?

I don't know. All I know is that she never grew round with child. She never laughed. And she stopped her prayers.

She should never have stopped her prayers.

In Egypt, there was a custom—a woman who failed to bear would be set aside, sent away, no longer a wife. But Abram kept her. And she kept me.

Then, after ten summers as the woman's maid-servant, everything changed. The day is etched in my mind. I had drawn water, brought it to the tent. She turned, looked at me. Studied me from my feet to almost my face. Her gaze never met mine. Instead, it rose to my neck and dropped again to my middle.

That middle grew cold. *Oh no . . .*

In ten summers, I had changed from child to woman.

"You are young," she said. She spoke in my presence, but it felt like she wasn't speaking to me at all. "There's a custom . . ."

A tremor ran through me. I knew the Canaanite custom, as I knew the Egyptian one. In Canaan, a woman could give her servant, her slave, to her husband as a concubine. And the child born would be credited to the wife. The servant could be used, and any child she bore taken from her and not counted as her own.

It was a horrible fate. Would it be mine?

The woman stood before me, her face hard. Then she exited the tent.

Trembling, I watched from behind the tent flap as she strode toward her husband.

"Behold now," she said. Her voice carried back to me on the breeze. "The Lord has prevented me from bearing children." I blinked. She had stopped her prayers, but she still blamed her god. She pointed back toward the tent where I stood in the shadows. *Don't. Don't say it.* But she did.

"Go in to my servant," she said to her husband. "It may be that I shall obtain children by her."

I dropped to my knees.

And Abram listened to the voice of his wife.

Of course he did. That night, he came to me. And the next night. And the next.

I had no choice.

And I hated the woman for it.

But then I conceived, and I hated her all the more.

I had lost my position as servant in Pharaoh's house, but now I began to believe I could have something more. I could be a wife. A real wife—with position, safety, and security in the household of this rich foreigner.

I should be the wife. Not her. I conceived. Not her. In Egypt, she would have been sent away, banished, stripped of her position. She had given up the title of *wife* easily enough there, and we had all paid the price. In the ten years since, she had not conceived.

But I had.

So I despised the one he called wife. And I let it show. I used words worse than *barren*. I called her names more stinging than a dried-up, old woman. I did not fetch the water. I did not cower. I did not obey.

I wanted her to pay for all the harm done to me. For every terrible thing that ever happened to me at her hands. She spied Abram and stormed from the tent, the words of my derision and disgust trailing after her.

"May the wrong done to me be on you!" She spit out the words and threw them in Abram's face. "I gave my servant to your embrace, and when she saw that she had conceived, she looked on me with contempt. May the Lord judge between you and me!"

Now she called on her god? *Now* she trusted him?

I held my breath, waiting for Abram's reply. Would he defend me?

But Abram said, "Behold, your servant is in your power; do to her as you please."

What she pleased was to beat me. And when she did, I ran. I ran and ran, without knowing where I was going. I ran until I could run no more, and I collapsed by a spring of water in the wilderness.

I'd been a fool. I was not a wife. I was nobody. Nothing. Abram used me, then threw me away. Gave me back into the hands of that woman.

So I sat by the spring and wept until I had no more tears. What was I going to do? I didn't know my way back to Egypt. And even if I did, I couldn't get there. And what would I do if I did? A pregnant woman, wandering the desert. I was a fool who had run off carrying Abram's child.

Where was Abram's god now?

And then he appeared. A man, but not a man. Something more. Somehow I knew he was a messenger of God. Abram's God. And he had come to me. Me. A slave. A foreigner. A woman used and beaten and thrown away.

Could it be that I was seen? I was heard? That I mattered?

And he said, "Hagar, servant of Sarai, where have you come from and where are you going?"

"I am fleeing from my mistress, Sarai."

He gazed at me tenderly, then spoke words he knew I wouldn't want to hear: "Return to your mistress and submit to her."

I bowed my head. He called that woman my mistress. I had wanted to displace her. But this messenger, this angel, wanted me to submit. And perhaps, just perhaps, I could. Because somehow this God of Abram saw even a lowly maidservant. I nodded and turned to go.

But the angel wasn't finished. He smiled and spoke more words of God. "I will surely multiply your offspring so that they cannot be numbered for multitude." Impossible words. Beautiful words. If this God could see a slave girl, all things were possible with him. Even this: "Behold, you are pregnant and shall bear a son. You shall call his name Ishmael, because the Lord has listened to your affliction."

The angel left me, and I was filled with wonder. Truly, I have seen him who looks after me. So I called the name of Lord, the One who spoke to me, "You are a God of seeing." Because he saw me. He knew me. He cared.

I went back to Sarai. I served her. I bore my son, Ishmael, and true to the Lord's promise, Ishmael was *my* son, not hers. My heart was full with love and pride. I would do anything for that boy, even serve a fickle mistress. And Abraham loved his son—that was plain to see.

And all went well until, by some miracle, Sarah, as she was then known, became pregnant and birthed Isaac, a son of her own.

Abraham, his name was Abraham by then, made a great feast on the day Isaac was weaned. And Sarah saw me laughing. Everyone was laughing. But that didn't matter to her. "Cast out this slave woman with her son, for the son of this slave woman shall not be heir with my son Isaac," she told Abraham.

And I was cast out. Thrown away, both me and my son. Nowhere to go, nothing to do. No home to call my own. Again. Still.

Abraham sent us away with nothing but bread and an old skin of water. He could have afforded more. He had, after all, thrown a whole party that day. There was plenty of food, plenty of wine. But he gave me only dry bread and a single skin of water.

My son and I wandered in the wilderness of Beersheba until the water and food were gone and my hope had dried up and died.

Ishmael was weak then, near death from lack of water. So was I.

Where was Abraham's God now? Where was the God who sees?

I had my son lay under a bush, protected from the sun. His lips were cracked, his skin covered in dry dust. He closed his eyes.

I couldn't watch him die. I just couldn't. So I went and sat a long way off, as far as a man could shoot an arrow from his bow. So far that I couldn't hear his cries.

And there I wept. Again.

Where is the God who sees me? Where is the God who sees my son? I cried the words silently. Again.

"What troubles you, Hagar?"

I startled, looked around. No one stood near me. But I recognized that voice.

It came once more, as if from the heavens. "Fear not, for God has heard the voice of the boy where he is." God heard him? Even I was too far away. "Up! Lift up the boy, and hold him fast with your hand, for I will make him into a great nation."

It was as if scales fell from my eyes. The God who sees opened my eyes so I could see the well of water before me. I took my son, just as the Lord said, and I filled the skin with water and gave my son a drink. He revived. He thrived.

And God was with him. God stayed with him, with us, as we lived in the wilderness of Paran, and Ishmael grew into a man. A man who was heir to a promise given to me from God himself. A promise to make him into a great nation. A promise that was bigger than any dream I had ever dared to dream. *I will become a great nation.*

Despite all the evil done to me, despite the number of times I had been used, abused, and thrown away, I mattered. I mattered to the God who sees me, and who chose to love me anyway. I was important to him.

Used

So often we ignore Hagar's story, as if she were just a footnote in the story of Abraham and Sarah. As if she didn't matter much at all. Nobody cared about Hagar. Not Pharaoh. Not Abraham. Not Sarah. And sometimes not even today's theologians.

At every turn, Hagar was used as a commodity for the purposes and gain of others, and then thrown away. She was used not only by Sarai and Abram in the attempt to secure God's promise of a child on their own terms, but she was also used by Pharaoh, who most likely gave Hagar to Sarai after the disastrous "she's my sister" incident in Genesis 12. Her life was defined by a series of events in which her needs, her wants, her desires were not considered at all. She was given away to a foreigner by Pharaoh; she was given to a man sexually so she could bear a son that would not be her own; she was abused by her mistress; and then she was cast aside once that mistress no longer needed her. Foreigner. Sexual slave. Property to be used, abused, and thrown away.

She mattered to no one.

Except God.

God spoke to her personally, rescued her, redeemed her abuse. He treated this Egyptian slave woman with respect, love, and care. With value. And he made her line into a great nation, just as he promised. He did it not because Hagar was humble or faithful or somehow deserving. He did it because he saw her suffering and offered his grace to a woman everyone else had discarded. They left her homeless, husbandless, and helpless, but God lifted her up and transformed not only her desperate circumstances but also her mistakes when he led her into a future that was more than she could ever have imagined for herself.

God can do that for you, too. He can take the worst of what you've suffered—your most painful humiliations and even lifelong dehumanizing moments—and, despite your own bitterness, pride, anger, and resentment, he can redeem them, and you. That's what God does.

When others use us and leave us without a place of safety, without a home, God is with us. When the love and security of family is taken from us—which, in Hagar's time, was what it was to be husbandless—God sees and intervenes. When we feel helpless to provide for our own needs or the needs of others, God will not leave us bereft.

Homeless

Hagar was a foreigner, living with foreigners, in a country that was not her own. Nothing was hers. Even the tent she slept in, the bed the slept on, were not hers. They belonged to her owners, Abram and Sarai.

Ripped from her country, she did not have the protections of family, home, and a common culture. The customs were different, the foods different, the gods different. She was on her own and therefore vulnerable to any use and abuse her master decreed.

When her mistress chose to give her to Abram sexually, even the child was not supposed to be hers. She had nothing. No one. Her circumstances were not unusual for that time. Yet despite the cultural norm, God did not allow Hagar to be alone.

Contrary to Sarai's plans and the Canaanite customs of the day, Ishmael was never Sarai's. Every reference in Scripture indicates Hagar was accepted as his mother despite the pre-arranged plan. God overruled the whims of Hagar's users and gave her the status of mother, the highest status for a woman of that day.

And then God did more. Not only did he make her a mother, he also promised that a nation would come from her. "Up! Lift up the boy, and hold him fast with your hand, for I will make him into a great nation," God says to Hagar (Genesis 21:18). She who had no nation would birth one.

That's the kind of God we have. We have a God of wonder, a God who plans and prepares for us a beautiful future even when we're used, abused, and cast aside. He did it for Hagar. He can do it for you, if you trust him just enough to listen to his voice, his promises, his truth, more than your fears, your hurts, your hopelessness. Even when you have no place to call home; even when you have no one to call family.

Husbandless

For a moment, after she conceived, Hagar believed herself superior to Sarai. We can imagine that she wanted to be somebody. To matter. To have a place in society as a full wife, the better wife. The important one.

Except she wasn't. At least not in the eyes of Abram and Sarai. "And when she saw that she had conceived, she looked with contempt on her mistress" the Bible tells us (Genesis 16:4). Sarai's response to Hagar's bid for importance was swift. She went directly to Abram to complain. At that moment, Abram had the power to decide whether or not this woman he and Sarai had used for their own purposes—and with whom he had lain as if she were his wife—was indeed a wife to him or if she were only a maidservant. Abram's response was as swift as Sarai's: "Behold, your servant is in your power; do to her as you please" (Genesis 16:6). Pregnancy did not raise Hagar's status at all. Abram had no interest in protecting the woman who carried his son. He had no intention of giving her the title of "wife." So Sarai took out her anger on Hagar.

And when Hagar ran away, no one came after her, even though she carried the child that both Abram and Sarai wanted, the child Sarai plotted to gain, the child that Sarai was willing to give up her exclusive sexual relationship with her husband to attain. Now, Hagar was pregnant, alone, and uncared for by the father of her child.

She had nothing. No husband. No family. No one.

Except God.

Abram's God, not some Egyptian god, sent his messenger to a foreign slave girl who was pregnant because of someone else's shortage of faith and surplus of fear. To the world around her, she was nobody. She was disposable. But not to God. *El ro'i*, the "God of seeing," looked after her (Genesis 16:13).

When she was all alone and pregnant, God was there. Not to condemn. Not to shame. Not to say, "You deserve this." Instead, he came to bless. He came to redeem. He came to turn a horrible, hopeless situation into a miracle that reflected the wonder of a God who loved Hagar, a slave, just as much as he loved Sarai, an heir to his covenant promise.

And all she had to do was obey God. He told her to go back and submit to her mistress. She was not to go back and vie for position; she was not to go back and try to be Abram's wife; she was simply to return and take the position assigned to her and do it well, do it right. And it seems that she did. And we never hear of her being abused by Sarai again. The relationship between her and Sarai remained adversarial, but we don't see Hagar treated harshly. She gave birth to a son Abraham cared about. Her son was her own, and she was not alone.

So, does this mean that God expects us to return and submit ourselves to the ones who used us? Emphatically, no. It does not. To use Hagar's story to assert such a thing would be a terrible mishandling of the text, a violation of the beauty of what God did for Hagar in appearing to her and providing for her needs. God did not send Hagar back because women need to submit to abusers. He sent her back because she was pregnant and alone and she would be cared for upon her return. Her return was a provision for her, a way for her to be safe. He sent her back to save her. In those days, no one else would have cared for a pregnant woman. And she and her baby could not have survived on their own. So God provided a way.

But in doing so, he asked her not to become an abuser herself. She was not to demean Sarai, who was also loved by God. She was not to dominate and discredit another woman upon whom God had placed his favor.

God did not say to return to Abram, the man, but to Sarai. Hagar was not meant to be the wife of Abram. It was not her place to displace Sarai. Abram was never a husband to her. He impregnated her and then ignored her. In fact, there's no indication that Abram ever had intercourse with Hagar after she conceived Ishmael. He took no responsibility for her at all.

But God did. He went after her as a husband would, he cared for her as a husband would. He made her the mother of multitudes, as a husband would.

God saw her, had always seen her. In fact, we see more instances in Scripture of God speaking with Hagar than of God speaking with Sarah! And he had a beautiful plan for the bitter, hopeless woman whom everyone else used and cast aside. Not because she had great faith (she didn't). Not because she was good and kind (she wasn't). Not because she was humble and obedient (she wasn't that either). She simply responded to God when he showed up. And she was blessed despite the abuse she suffered and the mistakes she made. Not because she was great, but because God is.

The God of whom Hagar proclaimed, "You are a God of seeing," is the same God who loves and looks after you today. You are not alone. You matter. You are treasured and precious. And you are the recipient of God's promises of hope, honor, and redemption. Like Hagar, your worth is not tied to your position in the world, by what's been done to you, or even by your own bitterness, failures, or anger.

God sees you. God comes after you. God loves you and promises a future as *his* wife, as *his* beloved. You matter to him. Even when you have no husband to care for you, no family to make you feel secure. Even when you feel like what you have been through has left you helpless and alone.

Helpless

Years after Ishmael was born, Sarah had a son, Isaac, the son of the promise, the one they'd all been waiting for. When Isaac was weaned, Abraham threw a big party to celebrate. In those times, weaning was an indication that a child would most likely live. Up to that point, a baby's survival was tentative. Until the weaning ceremony and celebration, Ishmael was still the back-up plan. But once Isaac was weaned, he was fully embraced as the fulfillment of God's promise. Which meant Ishmael, as well as Hagar, were no longer needed.

After twenty-five years with Abraham and Sarah, Hagar and her son were thrown out. Abraham, who had provided a feast the day before for everyone celebrating Isaac's weaning, provided only bread and a skin of water for Hagar and Ishmael. That was it. Bread, one skin of water, and nowhere to go. No help, no consideration, no concern.

Of course, the food ran out. Then the water ran out too. Ishmael became so dehydrated that he was near death. And Hagar was helpless to do anything about it. So she put her only son under a bush and sat down far enough away so she didn't have to watch him die. She had no hope, but God was with her, as he always had been.

This "God who sees" opened her eyes to see—not just the answer to her physical need but his personal care for her. She saw a well. But she also saw a God who cared enough to help her, to be with her in her distress, and to provide for her.

Beloved

Something wondrous happened right when Hagar felt the most helpless, when she had nowhere to go and no one to turn to. It was precisely then that God set her free from her lifelong slavery. The casting out that had seemed like a death sentence instead became a liberation. She was her own woman, a free woman, who would be the mother of multitudes, and God was with her. Always.

"And God was with the boy, and he grew up," the Scripture says. "He lived in the wilderness of Paran, and his mother took a wife for him from the land of Egypt" (Genesis 21:20–21). This woman who had no country, God made into the mother of a great nation. This woman who had no husband and was used sexually, God set free and stayed with her through her lifetime. To this woman who was all alone, helpless, without hope, without a future, God gave a heritage.

God longs give you an amazing future, too—no matter your past, no matter what others think, no matter how you've been used. God does not abandon you. The God who sees, who looks after you, can open your eyes to new hope, new freedom, and a new vision of what life can be. Because when you feel the most helpless, when all your options seem gone, when you've been used and cast aside, it is often at that very moment that God is working not just to save you, but to liberate you—to set you truly and fully free.

Because you are his beloved.

Who Is God When We're Used?

It fills me with hope that God cared so deeply for a woman who was a foreigner, not part of the covenant promise, and who didn't even behave admirably all the time. What kind of God sees and loves a foreign slave girl whom everyone else used and discarded? The answer: The kind of God who would one day choose to become homeless, family-less, and even helpless in order to make us his own.

The apostle Paul writes, "Though he was God, [Jesus] did not think of equality with God as something to cling to. Instead, he gave up his divine privileges; he took the humble position of a slave and was born as a human being. When he appeared in human form, he humbled himself in obedience to God and died a criminal's death on a cross" (Philippians 2:5–8 NLT).

Jesus chose to become a baby born in a barn, to be a wandering rabbi in our world, to be beaten and abused, to be thrown out on a cross to die. He did it for you and for me, he did it for everyone who has ever been used and thrown out.

When you feel homeless, he gives you his home. When you feel you have no family, he welcomes you into the family of God. When you feel helpless and alone, he is with you and he is your help. And when you feel you have nothing, remember: he became nothing, nobody, so you could receive the greatest promises of all—an eternal home, an eternal family, and an eternal life of love where every tear will be wiped away.

No matter what you have suffered, no matter how badly you've responded to your pain, the truth is that you are:

Not defined by being used . . . You are renewed.

Not defined by being abused . . . You are redeemed.

Not a nobody . . . You are God's own child.

Not discarded . . . You are precious and beloved.

And you will experience a whole different kind of "use." As a woman set free, no longer a slave to her past, you will be used to display God's mercy, his glory, his love, his wonder.

God will find you in the wilderness, and you will be used to bring hope to the hurting, much as Hagar's story brings us hope today. God will make you his own, and you will be used to reflect all the beauty of the God who loves you and will never cast you aside.

> And behold, I am with you always, to the end of the age.
>
> Jesus, Matthew 28:20

4

LOT'S DAUGHTERS AND A LEVITE'S CONCUBINE

Abused

Genesis 19; Judges 19

Such a horrible crime has not been committed in all the time since Israel left Egypt. Think about it! What are we going to do? Who's going to speak up? (Judges 19:30 NLT)

To be abused is to suffer cruel, violent, demeaning, or invasive treatment. Sometimes what we endure at the hands of others is so horrific, so harmful, that it seems we will never recover, never be ourselves again. Abuse often makes us feel less than, confused, afraid to trust *anyone*, afraid to believe that we are precious and valued in God's sight.

— · · · —

The story of Audrie Pott turns my stomach, sends shivers up my spine. I watch the Netflix documentary *Audrie & Daisy* on the big screen. How could these things happen? Still? And not only do they occur, but they are splashed over social media. She was just fifteen, raped repeatedly through the night by those who called themselves her friends. Covered in permanent marker, with the word "Here" and an arrow pointing to her private parts. Driven back to her home and thrown on the lawn. Treated like trash. I want to look away, I can't look away. Not even as the story tells of this beautiful girl's suicide just days later. Abuse, destruction, death. It's all so evil, so sickening.

I want to look away. I mustn't look away. I must see the horror so I can cry out for justice. And more than justice, for righteousness. I must cry out for change in a world in which these things can happen, do happen. Just as they always have.

I have to believe that we can do better than this. That we can face the abuse and injustice so we can fight for dignity, honor, decency—for the healing not just of a person but of a nation. A world.

As I sit in the theater trembling with revulsion, I think of other women who endured such abuse. And I remember that this culture of cruelty is not new. Before Israel even became a nation, women suffered horrendous violence and mistreatment. And I wonder, if these women could speak to us now, what would they say? How might they shine their light on a world gone wrong?

What would Lot's daughters say? What would a Levite's concubine say, one who died on a doorstep after a night of violent abuse?

If we let these women speak, perhaps their stories might sound something like this . . .

LOT'S DAUGHTERS SPEAK OUT

We shouldn't have been surprised. It was the way of things. But when our father brought the men, the strangers, into our home, we didn't know they would change everything. They seemed strong, noble, nothing like the men of Sodom. Father called for a feast. Mother kneaded dough. We baked unleavened bread and ate. But before the men lay down for the night, other men came to our door. The men of Sodom. All of them it seemed. They beat on the door with fists and blunt objects. I grabbed my sister's hand. Together we trembled. A voice boomed from outside the door. "Where are the men who came to you tonight? Bring them out to us, that we may know them."

Know them. It's a euphemism they use to soften the horror of rape.

Father glanced at us and the men who stood near us. Then he slipped out the door and shut it swiftly behind him. He spoke to the crowd, his tone wheedling. "I beg you, my brothers, do not act so wickedly." He paused.

We waited.

And he spoke again. "Behold, I have two daughters who have not known any man. Let me bring them out to you, and do to them as you please. Only do nothing to these men, for they have come under the shelter of my roof."

Oh no. I gripped my sister's hand tighter. Our eyes met. *Oh, God, no.* They would kill us. They would violate us until we were dead. How could our father say such things? How could he offer us up to a fate worse than any death?

Hospitality was important to my father, to us. It was a custom that should never be broken. Offer hospitality. Ensure safety. Give a feast. Give a bed. Guests before family. Men before women. But this—this was more than we could bear. Bile rose in my throat until I could barely breathe. Why did my father ever move to this hateful city? Why did he promise us in marriage to men who lived here? Why did he offer his own daughters to the most wicked men of this place where we'd made our home?

Were we worth so little to him? My gaze met that of my mother. But she stayed silent. Then she turned away.

God help us! No one else will.

My breath came in rapid gasps as my sister pulled me into her arms, and we waited.

"Stand back!" the vile voices of Sodom roared again. "This fellow came to sojourn, and he has become the judge! Now we will deal worse with you than with them." They pounded on the door. Then came a louder thump, as if they had shoved our father against the frame.

The men with us stepped forward. What would they do? Would they throw us out the door to be raped and mutilated? I trembled. My sister trembled more.

But the men moved around us. They wrenched open the door, grabbed our father, and yanked him inside. Then they slammed the door in the face of the men of Sodom.

Our guests made a swift gesture with their hands. Then shouts came from outside. "I can't see!" "Where's the door?" Bodies crashed against the sides of the house, but not against the door. For an hour, we waited through more shouts, the sound of men fumbling about, hitting our home. And finally, the noises faded and then vanished.

My sister leaned toward me. "Are they gone?"

The men, the angels, turned to our father. "Have you anyone else here? Sons-in-law, sons, daughters, or anyone you have in the city, bring them out of the place. For we are about to destroy this place, because the outcry against its people has become great before the Lord, and the Lord has sent us to destroy it."

Does the Lord hear? Does the Lord see? Did their words mean that our God cared about wickedness? Cared about us, even the women? Even the daughters? Father would have thrown us out to save strangers.

But would God save us?

Morning dawned. The angels arose. "Up!" they said to our father. "Take your wife and your two daughters who are here, lest you be swept away in the punishment of the city."

My sister and I stuffed small sacks with a few of our belongings.

Father lingered. Did he really want to stay longer in a city that would have brutalized his daughters?

The men seized him, and us, by the hands, opened the door, and hurried us from the city. "Escape for your life," one said. "Do not look back or stop anywhere in the valley."

So we ran, and fire and sulfur rained down on Sodom. Judgment. For all the evil those men had done, and for all evil they intended to do.

We could have died. But the Lord brought us out of evil.

A LEVITE'S CONCUBINE SPEAKS OUT

I know the story of Lot and his daughters. It happened almost a thousand years before I was born, yet I know what happened when the men of Sodom charged the door of Lot's home. I grew up with the story. We all did. I just never thought such a thing could happen in Israel.

A Levite came to Bethlehem and took me for himself. Though he would be considered my husband, I was merely his concubine, not his wife. I might have stayed with him if I'd been his wife, or even if he'd been kind. But I wasn't. And he wasn't. I was just property to be used in any way he wished. Sometimes he wished to ignore me. And sometimes he wished to be harsh.

So I ran away, back to Bethlehem, back to my father's home.

Weeks turned to months. I assumed he didn't care that I had left him.

But then, after four long months, he came after me with his servant and a couple donkeys. And he spoke kindly to me. That was new. Maybe, I dared to hope, things would be different now.

So I brought him into my father's home and imagined that now I could be his wife, not just a concubine. My father was so glad to see him. They ate and drank and spent five days together. My father didn't want him to go. I was glad for that. I felt valued in my father's home. A daughter and not just a possession, like a cow or sheep.

But the man refused to stay longer. On the evening of the fifth day, he left and took me with him. I longed for my father's home. I longed for my family. But maybe I would be a wife now. More than a possession. A respected position. Perhaps he would even continue to speak kindly.

With hopes scampering around in the shadows of my heart, I followed my sort-of husband as we neared Jebus and darkness started to descend. The servant wanted us to stop there for the night, but my master insisted we travel farther, to Gibeah, so we would not stay with foreigners but with our own people.

We would be safe with our own people.

We reached Gibeah, home to the tribe of Benjamin. But no one took us in for the night, so we sat down in the open square of the city.

It was strange. Someone should have welcomed us. Someone should have brought us into the safety of their home. Instead, we waited in the square as the darkness deepened.

Finally, an old man shuffled toward us. It appeared he was just coming home from work in the fields. "Where are you going, and where do you come from?" he asked as he drew near.

My master answered him. "We are passing from Bethlehem in Judah to the remote parts of the hill country of Ephraim, from which I come. I went to Bethlehem in Judah, and I am going to the house of the Lord, but no one has taken me into his house. We have straw and feed for our donkeys, with plenty of bread and wine for ourselves. There is no lack of anything."

The old man nodded. "Peace be to you; I will care for all your wants. Only, do not spend the night in the square."

I breathed a sigh of relief as he brought us into his house and gave the donkeys feed. His servants washed our feet, and we ate and drank. We learned that he also was from Ephraim.

All seemed well, just as it should be.

And then the horror began.

Men of the city surrounded the house. They beat on the door and shouted, "Bring out the man who came into your house, that we may know him." *That they may rape him.*

The old man called out, "No, my brothers, do not act so wickedly; since this man has come into my house, do not do this vile thing. Behold, here are my virgin daughter and his concubine." He motioned toward me as my heart turned to ice in my chest. "Let me bring them out now. Violate them and do with them what seems good to you, but against this man do not do this outrageous thing."

Time stopped. No nightmare I had ever conceived came close to the reality that faced me now. My gaze traveled to the man who had taken me from my father's home, who had spoken to me kindly. I sought mercy in his eyes. I sought hope. I sought anything but the hard implacability that I saw there. This was worse than harsh words. This was . . . this was . . . I wished I had never left my father's home.

The men wouldn't listen to the old man, so my master, my not-husband, grabbed me by the arm. His fingers bit into my flesh. "Go." He shoved me toward the door.

"No, please. No. Don't." But my words meant nothing. It was as if he did not hear them.

He thrust me out the door and slammed it behind me.

And then the men attacked me. Like wolves they surrounded me, violated me, devoured me. All night. It wouldn't stop. They wouldn't stop. The soul-wrenching agony of their abuse. And I couldn't get away.

Only as the morning light began to peek over the horizon did they let me go. I was torn, broken, bleeding. I crawled back to the old man's door, every inch of me throbbing with pain and humiliation.

As my hands groped for the threshold, each breath came slower, shallower than the last. I collapsed there, unable to move. As if from a great distance, I heard my master's voice: "Get up, let us be going."

But I knew I would never get up again.

Abused

How could such things happen in Israel? How could they happen here, or anywhere?

A father offers to throw his two daughters into the street to be raped and killed in order to protect some strangers, some men. A woman not valued enough even to be offered marriage is thrown out for the same reason, murdered through a night of the most savage abuse. The stories, as I sit with them, make it hard for me to even breathe. I want to rush past them, close my eyes, and pretend such things aren't part of Scripture, aren't part of real life. But God asks me to look the horror in the face and somehow, someway, find redemption. *Even here, Lord?* In these stories of savagery and evil? Could there be a sliver of hope, of meaning? And if so, what might the stories of these women communicate to women today who have suffered extreme abuse? Could there be a glimpse of God's love even here?

In order to address these questions, we need to first understand something about the culture of the ancient Middle East, for some have argued that the Levite, that Lot, had no choice but to offer the women to the depraved men of the cities. Some have argued that culture explains away their choices, even if it doesn't excuse the abuse.

But is that really true? What is the role of culture? And what does God really think about these men, these women, and the times in which they lived?

Does Culture Excuse Abuse?

In the deserts of the Middle East, ancient travelers were at risk from a host of threats, such as wild animals, bandits, thirst, starvation. Settlements were built around water sources that travelers needed to survive. Therefore, essential customs of hospitality were developed to protect both sojourners and the communities they visited. They were good customs, helpful, a reflection of God's character and of his concern for the outcast, the wanderer, the vulnerable.

The customs, as strong as laws, dictated that upon entering a new community, travelers were to be welcomed and taken into someone's home. The host, then, was obligated to provide food, water, and shelter before sending the travelers on their way. The sojourners accepted this hospitality with an understanding that they would not harm the community through theft or destructive behavior. While under the host's roof, the travelers were protected from thirst and starvation. These customs were held in high regard and any attempt to breach them—by the traveler, host, or community—was a serious offense and sometimes even considered an act of war.

However, prostituting one's daughters or concubines was also a serious offense. A father's duty was to find suitable husbands for his daughters and upon doing so, he was to protect the exclusive husband-wife relationship. Once promised, his daughters were not to be sold, bartered, used, or given away. Breaking the betrothal covenant, or even the relationship between a man and his concubine, was an offense not only against the two who were betrothed but against the entire community. In Lot's story, his daughters had been promised to men of Sodom. The text calls these men his "sons-in-law." In the Levite's story, the father of the concubine welcomes the Levite and entrusts his daughter to him. He is called the man's "father-in-law." Both Lot's daughters and the concubine should have been protected by the customs and laws of marriage.

They were not.

Why?

Not because of the cultural laws of hospitality—those customs should have protected the concubine as well. Not because the culture condoned sacrificing women sexually— purity and virginity, the sanctity of marriage, was important in both time periods in the Middle East. The problem was that wickedness had so permeated the cultures that violence and sexual sin had become a norm. And it was women who paid the price.

Lot chose to live in Sodom, a city so wicked that the very travelers he housed were angels sent by God to destroy it, even before the horrible threat Lot's daughters suffered. The Levite thought an Israelite town would be safer than a pagan village. He was wrong.

Evil had become the cultural norm, first in pagan Sodom, and then even among the people of Israel. And yet, even cultural norms were no excuse for the wickedness of the men of both cities, and it certainly was no excuse for the abuse perpetrated by Lot, by the Levite—men who should have upheld God's laws.

There is zero excuse for abuse.

So, why does God allow it to happen at all? I don't know. I wish he didn't. But I do know that God is not blind. He is not silent. But neither is he a God who destroys a person, a culture, a city, a community at the first signs of sin. If he did, none of us would survive.

And yet, I also know that God does not excuse sin. There is no indication in either story that God viewed what happened in Sodom or with the Levite's concubine as "okay." There was no "boys will be boys." There was no "it's not as bad as it could be." There was only severe condemnation of what these communities had become.

God and the Reality of Abuse

Evil exists. Abuse exists. It has since the garden of Eden. But God has never condoned it. Sometimes he saves us from abuse, as with Lot's daughters, and sometimes he allows evil to have its day, or in the concubine's case, its night. But he never looks away. He never minimizes the horror. He is a God of both mercy and judgment. Of justice.

In the aftermath of what happened with Lot's daughters and the men of Sodom, Sodom and Gomorrah were completely destroyed. Fire from heaven obliterated both wicked cities. In the aftermath of the concubine's death, Israel was severely rebuked in a gruesome display. In an act of prophetic outrage, the Levite cut up the dead body of his concubine and sent the parts to all the areas of Israel to bring vivid attention to the evil that had permeated Gibeah.

It was gruesome. But no more so than the abuse and murder that had happened to the concubine. Now, at least, the nation could not look away. They could not make excuses. They could not turn a blind eye.

And that changed everything. Everyone who witnessed these events said, "Such a horrible crime has not been committed in all the time since Israel left Egypt. Think about it! What are we going to do? Who's going to speak up?" (Judges 19:30 NLT).

What happened to the concubine could not be ignored. And change came from it. All the Israelites came out and gathered, "as one man to the LORD at Mizpah." Four hundred thousand warriors gathered to "repay Gibeah of Benjamin for all the outrage that they have committed in Israel" (Judges 20:2, 10). Let that number sink in: *four hundred thousand*. Warriors rose up against their brother tribe to correct the evil. They asked for the men who committed the depraved act to be handed over to them. But Gibeah resisted, refused to give up the wantonly evil men who had abused and killed the concubine. So the men of Israel declared war on the entire city, to purge the evil from the land.

They spoke up. They acted. The city that housed the men and refused to give them up to justice was attacked, the men killed, and the city set on fire. God did not allow the abuse and death of the concubine to go unnoticed or unrecompensed. Her abuse mattered. Her death mattered. It changed the world around her. It no doubt saved countless other women from horrific abuse.

In God's view, how a society treats its most vulnerable members—women and children, even travelers—is the measure of its righteousness. God rains down justice. For Lot's daughters, who were subject to the threat of abuse, the wicked cities were destroyed, and their father was cast out. He lived in caves and was later essentially raped by his daughters so they could get pregnant. His disregard for them became theirs for him.

And the concubine who died on the doorstep? Her death brought about a cultural reckoning of just reform for the nation, her very body a chilling call to repentance and righteousness.

God cares deeply about every act of abuse that is suffered by his people. Daughters, concubines, women, you, and me. And even when he seems slow to act, he will never just let it go.

Who's Going to Speak Up?

God has not changed since Lot's daughters ran toward the hills. He has not become lax since a woman died on a doorstep. He does not shrug and turn away, nor does he overlook the abuse that happened to you or to other women and children in our society. And neither should we. It's time for the horrors to come to light. We cannot bury the victims, pretend nothing happened. We can't hide or draw back. No cover-ups, no excuses. Instead, we must face the horror and expose it. As the Levite did in the book of Judges, we must call this "abomination and outrage."

Just as the Israelites cried out to God for justice and asked what they must do to purge the evil from their culture, we must fight for repentance and righteousness. We have been called to the battle for such a time as this.

Abused women do not need to be ashamed. You do not need to be ashamed. I do not need to be ashamed. Instead, we can choose to be warriors who take a stand for what is right. We can pursue justice, and in doing so, be used by God to transform our homes, communities, nations, and the world.

Who Is God When We're Abused?

The stories of Lot's daughters and the Levite's concubine vividly illustrate that abuse is caused by the wickedness of others. Audrie Pott didn't deserve what happened to her, no matter if she drank too much, or dressed in a short skirt, or let her belly show, or went to a party, or . . . anything. There is nothing a person can do to *deserve* abuse. It is always the result of wickedness at work in the abuser, and it thrives in cultures that overlook evil.

God not only understands that, but he has become the abused to heal the abused. When Jesus was arrested, and the crowds cried out, "Crucify him!" he could have been just crucified. That was bad enough and would have satisfied the conditions for the forgiveness of our sins.

But Jesus didn't just die, he was tortured. He was savagely beaten and scourged on the orders of Pontius Pilate, who claimed he found no basis for the charge against him. Jesus was innocent. Pilate knew it, yet he acquiesced to the crowd out of fear, just as Lot had done, just as the Levite had done. And so Jesus was subjected to horrific abuse. The whip used to beat Jesus, a Roman flagrum, was designed to tear the flesh from the body of its victim. It was a short whip made of two to three leather straps connected to a handle. Bits of jagged metal or bone were attached to the straps. After the scourge, the victim would be left clinging to life, much as the concubine on the doorstep. Then death would come by means of the cross. Jesus endured that abuse so we could be healed. "With his wounds, we are healed," says the prophet Isaiah (Isaiah 53:5). Like the concubine, Audrie Pott was violently and repeatedly raped. She was abused and thrown away. She chose to end her life.

If only she had known that God himself had sacrificed his life so that she might find hope and healing even after horrific abuse. If only all of us who have suffered abuse remembered that we are not alone. We do not suffer alone. We do not heal alone. Jesus walks this path with us. And we walk together.

He can redeem. He can make new. His is the stirring cry that demands repentance. He is the one who raises up warriors to fight for justice. Don't give up hope. Jesus suffered abuse and died on a cross, but that was not the end of his story. On the third day, Jesus rose from the dead and triumphed over death.

Death, abuse, humiliation, pain no longer have the final say. Not in Jesus's earthly life, and not in yours either. In Jesus, because of him, life and hope can overcome the horrors of evil. Jesus's humiliation, abuse, and death—and his resurrection—makes a way for you, for any of us, to rise up in new life, to receive healing, to seek victory over darkness, to live with hope.

Jesus lives. And no matter what abuse you've suffered, you can live in wholeness too.

> Clouds and darkness surround us, yet Heaven
> is just, and the day of triumph will surely come,
> when justice and truth will be vindicated.
>
> Mary Todd Lincoln

5

TWO TAMARS
Rejected

Genesis 38; 2 Samuel 13

Then Judah . . . said, "She is more righteous
than I." (Genesis 38:26)

To be rejected is to be discarded. Denied love, acceptance,
attention, approval. Sometimes the rejection that comes
after abuse can seem more hurtful than the abuse itself.
Sometimes we endure the initial pain, only to find ourselves
enmeshed in a new kind of torment, one that threatens to
rob us of dignity, power, and worth.

— • • • —

He was a pastor's son, newly graduated from Bible school
and recommended by other churches he'd served in during

his school years. "Up and coming," they said. "On fire for the Lord," they proclaimed. "Dynamic." And so it seemed. He worked with the youth of the church, taught about righteousness, prayer, and Bible reading. He was supposed to be someone we could trust. He seemed to be. He said all the right words. Prayed all the right prayers. Spoke fervently. Worshipped passionately.

And seduced at least two underage girls in the youth group.

We discovered his sin only because when he was finished with one, he rejected her, spurning her for the other. Then, he was about to do it again until someone, finally, spoke up.

Someone dared to demand righteousness and risk ridicule for telling the truth.

For years, in different churches, he'd operated in the shadows of silence and assumption, wreaking not only physical and emotional damage but spiritual destruction as well. Whispers were squelched as rumors. Recommendations were written by higher-ups who didn't bother to speak to the youth with whom he worked. Everyone assumed. Everyone presumed.

Until one brave girl who had been rejected stood up and told her story. Until she remembered that rejection did not make her helpless after all.

Her claims were investigated, and the young man was arrested, but for at least two girls, the damage was done. Someone they trusted, a charismatic leader in their church, used them and then rejected them. Despised them, because each of them, in turn, became a reminder of his sin, of his own lack of moral character.

It's becoming a familiar story. Too familiar in the church. And the wreckage of faith that often follows is enough to make us feel helpless, hopeless. In the face of such rejection, how can we trust again? How can we even trust God?

Common questions. Understandable ones. But are we truly helpless against the devastation to our faith and to our lives? Are the girls who were used and then rejected by the youth leader condemned to a broken faith, a life of desolation? Or is there hope even when betrayal happens in the church and at the hands of those we trusted and respected as men of God?

What do the stories of women in the Bible say about abuse committed by men of faith? What does it say about the choices we have? The power we still have? Is there a path of righteousness, justice, and healing for those abused in the church?

Before you read further, be forewarned: This chapter might be disturbing. If your focus is to make sure that culpability is properly distributed, then you aren't yet ready to tackle the stories of two Tamars. This chapter is not about who's to blame and the shouldering of guilt. It's not about the assigning of fault.

It's about defying the assumption, the fear, that abuse makes us powerless, that there's nothing we can do but be resigned to our fate.

So, if you're sick of feeling helpless, if you're longing to move beyond questions of who did the right thing and who did wrong, if you're done pointing fingers and instead are determined to find the will to heal, to live in the wonder of God, to choose to be free, then read on. This chapter will be challenging, but at its core there is a fierce hope, a dogged commitment to the truth of Romans 8, that nothing—*nothing*—can separate us from the love of Christ. No matter what the culture says, no matter how loudly your fear screams that you are forever marred, no matter the self-deprecating whispers regarding our worth, Scripture teaches that God does not leave us powerless, voiceless, and without hope. God himself will provide a way to heal and redeem our brokenness. But we must dare to try.

If you're still reading, I believe that if we look at the stories of two Tamars, we can find the hope and encouragement we need to step into the strength God provides. We can discover that the choice between desolation and fierce faith does not belong to the one who betrayed faith, to the abuser, to the wrongdoer, but it belongs to the ones betrayed, to you and me, to those discarded by men but not discarded by God.

We are not powerless.

TAMAR SPEAKS OUT

They should have been better, all of them, followers of *El Shaddai* as they were. Judah took me as a wife for his firstborn, Er. But Er was wicked, and the Lord put him to death. So Judah gave me to Onan, his second son, as our God commands. But Onan refused to give me a child. Oh, he came in to me, he took me as a man takes a wife, but he would not allow me the dignity, the security, of a child. He spilled his seed on the ground. On the ground! So I was forced to endure him . . . for nothing.

I endured, and I prayed, and I waited.

And God saw. What Onan did was wicked in the sight of our God, and death took Onan too. I was a widow, twice over.

Judah had a third son. He was but a boy.

"Remain a widow in your father's house," my father-in-law told me, "till Shelah my son grows up." I took him at his word and then returned to my father's house to wait. The months stretched into years, and I grew older.

Shelah grew older too. Old enough to take a wife. Old enough for Judah to do what was right by me, what was required by God.

But no one ever came to call me back to Judah's house, to offer me in marriage to his son. Instead, Judah ignored me. He threw me away, forgetting his promises, forgetting our laws, our customs, denying me my rights.

Again, I endured, and I prayed, and I waited.

I wrestled with doubts, questions, fears: Should I accept this injustice done to me? Should I live forever as a desolate woman in my father's house? Could there be another way?

Would El Shaddai himself open a way of justice for me? And if he did, would I dare to walk in it?

Word came then that my father-in-law was coming to Timnah to shear his sheep. The road was not far from my father's home. I could meet him there. I could confront the father-in-law who did me wrong, who resigned me to a life of desolation when I was no longer convenient.

Would I accept this fate chosen by others? Would I hide away in my father's house and give up my hopes and dreams?

Or would I gather up my courage like a cloak and do something audacious and bold, claiming what was within my rights? If not my husband's brother, then his father could fulfill the family's duty to me so the family line would be preserved.

I took off my widow's garments and covered myself with a veil, wrapping myself in the cloth, covering my face as the cult prostitutes do. Then I sat at the entrance to Enaim, on the road to Timnah.

And I waited.

And lifted my chin.

And fought back fear.

Eventually, Judah came. He turned to me at the roadside. "Come, let me come in to you," he said to me. I clenched my jaw. He would dally with a cult prostitute, but not do right by his own daughter-in-law. This man, who claimed his father's, his grandfather's, his great-grandfather's God, who of all people should have done right, did not. Would not.

But I had a plan. It was risky. It could cost me everything. But sometimes you have to risk much for righteousness. For justice.

I drew a deep breath. And dared. "What will you give me, that you may come in to me?"

He answered quickly enough. "I will send you a young goat from the flock."

"Give me a pledge, until you send it."

"What pledge shall I give you?"

I took a deep breath. "Your signet and your cord and your staff that is in your hand." Things personal to him. Things he would recognize and could not deny were his.

He gave them to me, laid with me, and left.

I hurried back to my father's house, changed into my widow's garb, and hid Judah's things in my bedchamber.

Months passed, and I was pregnant. God provided through Judah what Judah had refused me. God had seen my plight, had blessed my boldness.

But of course, no one knew that. Instead, they believed me pregnant through immorality. And they told my father-in-law.

He would not come to my father's house to do right by me, to bring me to his son. But he was quick to arrive once my supposed sin was known.

"Bring her out, and let her be burned!" he declared.

I trembled as I pulled his personal items from their hiding place. I clutched them to my chest. I needed only a bit more bravery, a moment more of courage. As they brought me out, I sent word to my father-in-law. "By the man to whom these belong, I am pregnant," I said. My voice shook only a little. It was time. Time for justice. Time to reclaim the life taken from me. "Please identify whose these are, the signet and the cord and the staff."

I prayed and I waited yet again.

Finally, my father-in-law responded. "She is more righteous than I, since I did not give her to my son Shelah."

He declared my righteousness to all who stood by. He acknowledged it even over his own. I risked everything for what was right. And I won. There, in front of my father's house, I was called more righteous than a great-grandson of Abraham.

Peace washed over me. I was not desolate. I was not bereft. God had given me a future and a hope.

In due time, I gave birth to twin boys—my legacy and my redemption. I was not helpless in the face of the wrong done to me. Instead, I was justified and set free.

CENTURIES LATER, ANOTHER TAMAR SPEAKS OUT

I was named after her, you know. Tamar, my ancestor, who stood for justice, who demanded her due, fought for rectitude when it would have been easier to live in resignation. She dared. And she triumphed.

I did not.

My father was King David, lover of God, singer of songs, minstrel of the music of both praise and lament. We were supposedly a kingdom, a family, devoted to the service of our God. We knew what was right and wrong. We had the law. We had faith.

But . . .

It wasn't enough.

My half-brother, Amnon, thought he loved me. Love? Lust, maybe. He was certainly taken with my beauty. He made himself ill with his want.

But I was a virgin. I followed the ways of our God. As he should have.

But he was not used to the word *no*.

My father sent word to me at the palace one day. "Go to your brother Amnon's house and prepare food for him." I wondered. I worried, but I went. Surely everything would be fine, I thought. My brother is a man of God, and he knows the law.

He was lying down when I arrived. I took some dough, kneaded it, and made bread. I baked it, with him watching my every move. When the bread was ready, I emptied the pan before him, but he refused to eat. "Send everyone out of here," he said.

They left us. Alone.

"Bring the food here into my chamber, that I may eat from your hand."

So I brought it to him. In his bedroom.

I don't like to remember what happened next. I ask myself what I could have done differently. I review my thoughts, my actions, a thousand times. I just didn't think, I didn't believe, I would never have dreamed he would do what he did. Especially because he didn't have to. He could have asked for my hand. Our father would have given it to him.

But he didn't want that. He didn't want to wait. He didn't want to do things right.

"Come lie with me, my sister," he purred as he grabbed me, forcing me toward him.

Sister. He dared to call me his sister when all he could think of was his lust. That is no way to treat a sister.

I pushed against him. "No, my brother, do not violate me, for such a thing is not done in Israel; do not do this outrageous thing." But he didn't relent, so I struggled, and pleaded, and bargained. "As for me, where could I carry my shame? And as for you, you would be as one of the outrageous fools in Israel. Now therefore, please speak to the king, for he will not withhold me from you."

I spoke what was right and good, but he wouldn't listen to me. It would have been so easy, a simple request to the king. But he chose violence instead. He shoved me down and raped me.

Then, this man who was the son of the king, hated me with a hatred far greater than any love he had previously professed. "Get up! Go!" he sneered at me.

I trembled. Would he really violate me and then reject me? Would he not claim me now that he took what was precious to me? "No, my brother, for this wrong in sending me away is greater than the other that you did to me." But again, he did not listen. He had no ears for what was right.

He called his young servant and told him, "Put this woman out of my presence and bolt the door after her."

I ran then, as the bolt drew shut behind me. I tore the long robe I wore, put the ashes of grief on my head, and wept aloud as I stumbled back toward the palace.

My full brother, Absalom, met me. He told me not to take it to heart. How could I not? The pain went deeper than my heart, into my very soul. Then, he told me to hold my peace. And I did. That I did. I said nothing. I did nothing.

I simply let Absalom act for me. Think for me. Do for me. It seemed my only choice at the time. But now I wonder . . .

Two years, two long years later, he avenged my violation by murdering Amnon. He called it justice, but it was only revenge. It changed nothing. It did nothing. I was not vindicated. I was not redeemed. I was not healed. And I lived as a desolate woman, devastated, lonely, ruined, in Absalom's house all the days of my life.

And sometimes, in the dark of night, when the tears run dry, I wonder what my life might have held if I'd only followed my namesake's example and not given up hope.

What if I had believed that all was not lost when my virginity was stolen? What if I refused to be powerless in the face of my pain? What if I had trusted in the character of God more than the condemnation of my culture?

What if I dared to hope in my God?

Rejected

The two Tamars had vastly different responses to the injustices they faced, and then vastly different outcomes. As I read their stories together, I am amazed by the authority, the power to choose, that God gives to each of them. Both were treated wickedly. Both suffered gross injustice. Both were relegated to a life of desolation by circumstances outside their control. Neither provoked nor deserved the injustice that befell them. In their cultures, both, as women, had very few options and very little power. Both should have been helpless, hopeless, in the face of the unrighteous actions of supposedly godly men.

And yet . . .

While culture said that the men held all the power, it wasn't the circumstances of these women or the actions of others that ultimately defined their lives. God did not turn his back, leaving them helpless and hopeless. Rather, God gave each of them the power to choose desolation or hope. To remain helpless or to dare to try for justice. I love that! Our culture would say that we haven't any choice, that power belongs to the powerful. But God says no. He says that even those who seem powerless, even those who have been oppressed, used, abused, hurt, and rejected, have the power to choose to live in righteousness and hope. We have the power to believe that God loves us.

God gives us that choice, that power, even when injustice followed by disregard comes to us through men of faith. Even when we are told to "not take it to heart" and to "hold our peace." It's not easy. It's not a simple choice. It's always a risk, especially when we've been so deeply hurt. Will we dare to believe that God wants good for us, or will we let fear and pain keep us in desolation?

Remaining Desolate

Amnon was the firstborn son of King David, whom God called "a man after my heart" (Acts 13:22). Amnon would have been expected to take the throne, and was trained in the ways of God. In that culture, he could have had as many wives as he wanted. He could easily have taken his half-sister, Tamar, as a wife when he desired her.

But he didn't.

What is a woman to do when faced with this kind of injustice? What does she do when she is violated by someone she trusted? What if it's someone we'd consider "a man after God's heart" who wrongs her? What choice does she have when a Christian man, even a leader in the faith is the one who hurts, belittles, demoralizes, and demeans—or worse? What if it's another who violates her, and then a person of faith dismisses her pain, telling her to "hold her peace" and "not take this to heart"—what should she do?

Like Amnon's half-sister, we can choose to be resigned to our fate. We can give in to the pressure of family, society, the church, and "keep our peace," to not cause any trouble. Live with the pain alone while others tell us to not take what has happened to heart. We can creep away and hide ourselves behind walls, believe our life is ruined, and "live as a desolate woman" for the rest of our days.

Or we can choose otherwise.

I wonder what might have happened if Tamar had chosen to reject Absalom's advice to be silent and hold her peace. What if her encounter with Absalom had gone something like this instead . . .

"Has Amnon your brother been with you?"

"Yes. He has done what should never be done, especially by a follower of our God."

"He is your brother; do not take this to heart."

"What! I have been *violated.* God's righteousness has been violated. Of course, I will take this heart!"

"Hold your peace, my sister."

"No, my brother! I will not hold my peace. I will not live in desolation, helpless and hopeless, in your house while you scheme revenge. I am not who Amnon tried to make me to be, no matter what he did to me. I am a daughter of the king!"

I like that scenario better than what I read in 2 Samuel 13. Who knows what might have happened if Tamar had refused to let her rape define her. Maybe her situation would have been redeemed. Maybe her life would have been filled with new beginnings, radical blessing, shocking beauty. Maybe. We can't know because she didn't do that. It seems that she closed the door, Absalom's door, and kept it closed, silently accepting her desolate state . . . for the rest of her life.

When 2 Samuel 13:20 says, "So Tamar lived, a desolate woman, in her brother Absalom's house," the Hebrew indicates that she remained in a state of desolation. It wasn't a passing stage of grief. She settled there. Lived in that state. It is one thing to be desolate, to be sorrowful and inconsolable, for a time. Often we need time to grieve our losses, process the pain of what's been done to us. But to remain in desolation as a lifestyle is never God's will. Not for Tamar. And not for you.

Some may think that "desolate" here simply means that she remained childless, barren, but this Hebrew word, *shamem*, means "devastated" or "appalled." The basic definition of desolate indicates a state of bleak and dismal emptiness, of being destroyed by overwhelming grief. *The Expanded Bible* provides other possible ways of translating a particular word in Scripture that help us see a fuller picture of what is meant; it translates *shamem* as "sad and lonely [desolate and inconsolable]."

It is not uncommon either in the Bible or in modern times for a woman to be childless. However, God never intends for even the childless woman to live in this kind of desolation. We do not have to be overwhelmed by grief and without hope! This is *never* God's will for us.

So we are left to wonder what would have happened if Tamar had not resigned herself to desolation. What if she had not believed she was powerless, helpless, forever condemned to live in this state of sad loneliness and hopelessness? What if she had at least tried for justice, reached for hope, even if it was a week later, a month later, a year later? What if she had said no to the helplessness and believed that somehow, someway, God wanted more for her? What if she believed that God still cared about her?

But she "held her peace" instead.

It's an understandable choice, but a regrettable one none-theless. It's a choice we sometimes make as well. Sometimes we call it "forgiveness." But nowhere does the Bible indicate that forgiveness is anything like Absalom's advice to hold one's peace. It isn't not making a fuss. It isn't pretending that the abuse, the injustice, the sin didn't happen or didn't matter. Forgiveness is the opposite of what we see in Tamar's story. The Bible doesn't say, "Tamar forgave her brother and was set free." Instead, we read that Tamar lived in desolation *all her life*. And revenge was a poor substitute for justice when Absalom murdered Amnon.

God wants more than resignation for those who have been rejected and betrayed. He wants so much more for us than desolation. We don't have to pretend in order to make things easier for others, especially for those who abused and rejected us. We don't have to make what happened more palatable for our family, our friends, or those who know the offending party. We don't even have to make it more agreeable to those in the church.

Because God is a God of truth. And he is a God of justice. And most of all, he is a God of hope. And love.

What happened to Tamar was unjust and horrible and hurtful and traumatic and destructive. Absalom's offer to take her in and take care of the problem must have seemed like a mercy. She could withdraw, let him handle it. In her pain, and with the pressures of her culture that assumed she was forever "ruined," it must have seemed like a good choice, perhaps the only choice.

But it didn't lead to healing. It didn't allow God to work on her behalf, to heal and redeem her with his love. It allowed Absalom to seek revenge, which did nothing to change her situation—she remained desolate. Silence didn't heal her. Revenge didn't set her free. But perhaps a bold belief in the love of God, and a trust that he never leaves us powerless in pursuing what is right, what is good, would have.

She might have felt that resignation was the only response she could make to rejection. But there was a better way. A different way. For her—and for us.

A Better Way

Judah's daughter-in-law also suffered grave injustice at the hands of a man who was supposed to be a follower of God. Today, it may seem that the injustice she suffered wasn't nearly as severe as what happened to Tamar, her descendant. After all, she was merely sent back to her father's house to grow old. It doesn't sound so bad. And there's no evidence she suffered any physical violence. But in her culture, Judah's refusal to give her a husband was just as damaging to her future as Amnon's sexual attack. Judah's action consigned Tamar to the exact same fate as her descendant—a life that was without hope, without a future. A life that could have been one of desolation, sorrow, and loneliness. Children secured a woman's future in those times. But both Judah and Amnon denied that promised future to the respective Tamars.

Amnon's half-sister believed culture over the character of God.

Judah's daughter-in-law did not.

Instead, the first Tamar watched for an opportunity to make things right. The Bible gives no indication that she wasted any effort considering revenge. Rather, when she saw that the cultural and moral law that should have protected her was not being followed, she chose to try to pursue what was just, at significant risk to herself. I believe she did it because she knew who she was, and she knew what was right. As a widowed daughter-in-law, she was entitled to the promise of children through the brothers of her first husband, to secure her future and the lineage of the eldest son. Judah's unrighteous choices did not change her view of herself. She did not believe she was no longer worthy of her rights as widow. She could have chosen to believe there was something wrong with her and that was why she didn't deserve to be treated well and given in marriage to Shelah as promised. But she didn't. There is no indication in the text that she felt less than, worthless, disgraced, contemptible, or undeserving. In fact, her actions tell us just the opposite. She believed, strongly enough to risk death, that she deserved to be treated with justice and respect.

And so, when Judah denied her rights as a woman and widow, she also didn't believe she was forever condemned to that fate. When the opportunity arose for her to step forward and risk all, she was ready. She removed her widow's clothes and dared to confront the source of her injustice in a way that required fierce courage.

She laid a trap for Judah.

Our modern sensibilities are often offended by what she did. She dressed like a prostitute! She had sex with her father-in-law! Surely, God didn't condone her actions. Surely what she did was a sin! But notice that Tamar never lied to Judah. She didn't say she was a prostitute; that was his assumption. She didn't beckon him in, call to him. She simply put herself in a position to receive justice.

In Tamar's culture, it was acceptable for her to sleep with her father-in-law to gain a promised child through his line. He should have given her to Shelah, as both culture and law dictated (and the Law of Moses would later confirm in Deuteronomy 25:5), and as he promised he would, but he didn't, and so her actions were not considered immoral. In fact, even Judah recognized her righteousness in tricking him into doing right. Later, Israelite laws would forbid lying with a close relative (Leviticus 18), but the law would continue the tradition of a childless widow becoming the wife of her husband's brother in order to continue his lineage. That law persisted through the centuries and is even mentioned in the Gospels (Matthew 22; Mark 12; Luke 20).

Might there have been a better plan than changing her dress and waiting at the roadside for Judah? Might she have done something that seems to us to be more righteous? Perhaps. But it's important to notice that the text never condemns her actions, never questions them or places them in a negative light. Judah called her "righteous" and honored her.

Choices

Both Tamars were discarded, both pressed to destitution, both treated horribly, both hurt, both abandoned, both rejected by men who should have known better, been better. The key difference between Judah's daughter-in-law and Amnon's half-sister was not so much that the first Tamar pursued action (she didn't for many years), but rather that Judah's actions didn't change her view of herself or what she knew to be right. She knew who she was and how she should have been treated. She never wavered in that conviction. And so she was ready to take action when the opportunity arose. She did not resign herself to desolation, believing that she had no hope and no recourse. She didn't allow self-pity, self-guilt, self-blame to shape her identity or her ability to pursue what was right. She simply worked to put herself in a position for God to work, despite her pain and the risk involved.

And God blessed and honored her.

She not only birthed children, as should have been her right as a wife of Er, Onan, and then Shelah, but her son, Perez, became an ancestor of King David, and therefore of Jesus himself.

It was not the injustice but her *response* to the injustice that determined her future. She didn't give up hope. She didn't resign herself to helplessness.

We have that same power to choose hope, to choose life, and to trust in the righteousness and love of God. The fact is, people sin. Men who are supposed to be better sin too. Men we trust. Spiritual leaders. Just like Judah, just like the sons of David. We do not have to allow the hurt, the wrong, the sin of others, to define our future, or to define our status as beloved children of God. The injustices done to us do not have to determine our fate or our opportunities. We can choose to boldly believe that God loves us fiercely. We can choose to believe that he will work for righteousness on our behalf, no matter how much time has passed.

Your commitment to God's love for you and to his view of your worth, even when it seems you have little power, is all God needs to begin working redemption for you. He wants to give you a future colored by joy and promise. But first, you must refuse to be consigned to a destiny determined by others.

We don't have a choice in our abuse, but we do have choices about what happens next. God gave both Tamars a choice. He gives you choices too. For those who choose to hide and believe they are ruined, desolation waits in the shadows. But for those who choose to step forward and dare to embrace God's love and righteousness, dare to embrace their standing as beloved by God, there is blessing. God will strengthen, and he will lead into a future of hope and redemption.

Who Is God When We're Rejected?

God is especially concerned with those who have been hurt and rejected. Five times New Testament writers quote the words of Psalm 118:22: "The stone that the builders rejected has become the cornerstone." Jesus refers to himself as that rejected rock. And the religious leaders of his day were the "builders" who rejected him, rejected their Messiah, the Savior. But despite their rejection, Jesus became the cornerstone, the stone upon which the building rises and finds its strength. He knows what it means to be thrown away by those calling themselves religious. And God knows how to build with strength on that rejected stone. He knows how to build beauty, purpose, and wonder out of your life too.

In Luke 14, Jesus tells a beautiful parable that reveals God's heart for the rejected and the outcasts. When a master threw a great banquet and those he first invited made excuses and didn't come, he said to his servants, "Go out quickly to the streets and lanes of the city, and bring in the poor and crippled and blind and lame." When there were still empty seats, the master said, "Go out to the highways and hedges and compel people to come in, that my house may be filled." God doesn't merely set aside a few extra seats in case someone wanders by, he actually searches for those who have been rejected. He welcomes the spurned to his great banquet. He welcomes you, and me. We have only to accept the invitation.

Come to the feast. Embrace what's right even when what happened to you is so wrong. The Savior who was rejected is calling you to join him and hide no longer. He who is faithful and true (Revelation 19:11) is searching for you, calling you to join the feast, to receive the good news that you are wanted and welcomed into his love.

The two underage girls who were seduced and rejected by the youth leader had the same invitation. One withdrew from her faith, blamed God, believed that if she couldn't trust a man who was supposed to be godly, she couldn't trust God either. But the other girl, she continued in her faith. She believed God would heal her, believed he condemned the wrong done to her even more strongly than she did. She dared to believe that she mattered to God and that what happened to her was wrong. She didn't deserve it. And she wasn't ruined. For her, embracing righteousness meant that she had to testify in court. It won't mean that for everyone. But for her, it was a way to come out of hiding and reject helplessness. And she thrived. It was still hard, it still hurt, but she is on her way to healing.

What about you? Will you dare to trust God? Will you dare to take a risk and believe that God does not want you to be joyless, lifeless, hopeless, no matter what happened to you? Will you dare to come to the feast of the Lamb, even when wrong was done to you by someone who claimed faith in Christ?

Sometimes the first step is simply to acknowledge what happened by sharing it with a trusted friend. You say aloud that it wasn't right. It wasn't your fault. You did not deserve it. Sometimes the first step is remembering who you truly are in Christ—that you are precious, beloved, and no amount of breaking, betrayal, or rejection, makes you matter less to him. And sometimes, you have to confront your abuser.

God will guide you, if you dare to trust him and believe in his love for you. His invitation is always open. It's open to you now. It's time to come out of hiding and say yes to the One who will never reject you. It's time to no longer be made desolate by fear.

It's time to stand up and embrace the hope and love of God.

> Therefore take up the whole armor of God, that you may be able to withstand in the evil day, and having done all, to stand firm.
>
> The apostle Paul (Ephesians 6:13)

6

HANNAH

Devalued

---

1 Samuel 1–2

Then the woman went her way and ate, and her
face was no longer sad. (1 Samuel 1:18)

Devalued. Degraded. Diminished. Debased. Not all dehumanizing situations are about sexual abuse. Some
center on being devalued for who we are, for not meeting others' expectations or fitting into traditional roles for women.
For being too much or not enough.

--- • • • ---

What do we do when we just don't fit? When value is based
on how well we conform to expectations, how closely we
adapt to a preset mold?

In college, I was active in a Christian group, but never invited to advanced training conferences. Why? "You aren't ever going to be a leader, are you?" they said. I didn't fit their idea of a female leader. Later, I struggled with a new editor for one of my books. Why? I didn't fit his idea of what a female writer should be. After that, I faced decades of infertility, and groaned under the added weight of not measuring up to what my culture said a woman had to be in order to be of value. Could I be a woman and not a mom?

But when I read through the biblical stories, I discovered a woman named Hannah who didn't fit either. She wasn't what her culture thought she should be. And it hurt. It hurt so badly that she wept in the temple to the point of appearing to be drunk.

I wonder, what might Hannah say if she could speak to women today who don't fit the mold? How would she encourage us?

Perhaps she might say something like this . . .

HANNAH SPEAKS OUT

I want to be like everyone else. I want children just like everyone else. But the Lord has closed my womb. So I am different and, according to Peninnah, my husband's other wife—his fertile wife—I am less. Worth*less*. Use*less*. A poor excuse for a woman.

Every year, we go up to Shiloh to worship and sacrifice to the Lord of hosts. Every year, it's the same. Elkanah, my husband, gives portions of the sacrifice to Peninnah and all her sons and daughters. She is just what a wife should be—the mother of many. It seems she is always pregnant or nursing.

And I remain un-pregnant, never nursing. Elkanah gives me a double portion because he loves me. But even he must know it's not enough, especially with the taunts of my rival.

The mocking grows worse every year, culminating on the day of sacrifice. Peninnah flaunts her children and derides my barrenness, my differentness. She does it to hurt me, to hate me. As if I don't know how I've failed to be a proper wife, a proper woman, a mother. As if I don't know that it's the Lord who has closed my womb for reasons I cannot fathom, cannot begin to understand.

On and on, she taunts, provoking me so mercilessly that I cannot eat even one portion of the sacrifice, let alone the two that Elkanah gives me.

So I weep and do not eat. My husband doesn't understand. "Hannah, why do you weep?" he says to me. Why? Because I am forgotten by the Lord. Because I am less than, I am useless. Because I cannot escape the pain of Peninnah's taunts. Even when she is silent, the words still worm their way into my soul, whispering, hissing, shouting all the things everyone says I should be, and all I am not.

But Elkanah can't hear the voices. "And why do you not eat?" he continues. "And why is your heart sad? Am I not more to you than ten sons?"

Ten sons. Does he not know that in our culture, and in our household, a woman's worth is based on the number of her sons, not on the love of her husband?

And in my pain, my husband, who loves me, also chides me. Isn't he enough? Isn't his love enough to satisfy my soul?

It isn't. Was it ever meant to be?

The others eat. They drink. I poke at my food, my stomach roiling with sorrow.

When they finish their meal, I rise. I stumble toward the door of the temple. Eli, the priest, sits beside the doorpost. I avoid him, falling to my knees in the shadows, tears blurring my vision.

I kneel in the Lord's house. What if nothing ever changes? What if I continue to come here year after year to be mocked by Elkanah's other wife. What if my life never becomes what I dream for it to be? What if I am always going to be different?

What if God never remembers me?

I continue to weep, to cry out in my heart to God. And in my heart, I feel a movement. A change.

Does he hear me? And what would I ask if I knew my words were heard by my God?

I know this much, at least: I have no one, no hope, but in him.

As I weep and pray, I hear the whisper of a question. I feel a prodding in my soul. *Do you really want to be like Peninnah?*

I've always thought so, yes. And yet, do I truly want to be just like everyone else?

My soul shivers.

What if I dared to peek beyond my dreams of having as many sons as my rival? What if I dared to look past the picture of the woman, the life, I've assumed I wanted, and see what God may have for me instead?

What if . . .

I wonder.

O, Lord of hosts, if you will indeed look on the affliction of your servant and remember me and not forget your servant, but will give to your servant a son, then I will give him to the Lord all the days of his life, and no razor shall touch his head.

A bargain? Not really. But a pledge. A pledge to look beyond myself to my God. To look beyond my dreams and to instead embrace his. To dare to be different, even if my prayers are answered.

I continue to pray, my lips moving, my voice silent.

The priest rises, comes over to me. "How long will you go on being drunk? Put your wine away from you."

I look up, trembling. Drunk? Wine? Will he, too, mock me in my pain? Can a woman not pour out her heart to her God without suspicion, without a man thinking she is a fool? My pain, interpreted as drunkenness. My broken heart, rebuked as if I've drowned it in wine.

"No, my lord, I am a woman troubled in sprit. I have drunk neither wine nor strong drink, but I have been pouring out my soul before the Lord. Do not regard your servant as a worthless woman, for all along I have been speaking out of my great anxiety and vexation."

Do not demean me over my pain. Do not devalue me because I hurt.

He looks at me for a long moment, this priest of the Lord, this man who is supposed to speak for God and not for himself. He nods once. "Go in peace, and the God of Israel grant your petition that you have made to him."

The peace he speaks of washes over me, and I know it is from the Lord of hosts. Real peace. I have not been forgotten. I have been heard. The Lord has listened to my plea. He has blessed his servant. "Let your servant find favor in your eyes," I say, looking at the priest, but I am saying it to God.

I am his servant. I always will be.

And suddenly, even though I have no child, I find that knowing my God has heard me is enough to satisfy my soul.

Devalued

In due time, Hannah became pregnant and gave birth to a son. She called him Samuel, which in Hebrew sounds like the word for "heard of God." She was heard, she was remembered, and she fulfilled her vow. As soon as Samuel was weaned, she brought him back to Eli, the priest. She sacrificed there and, as she promised, gave her son to the Lord. "Therefore I have lent him to the LORD. As long as he lives, he is lent to the LORD," she said (1 Samuel 1:28).

Samuel grew to be one of the greatest prophets of Israel. He anointed their first king, Saul, and anointed David as their second king as well. He became instrumental in the history of Israel and the history of our salvation. All because Hannah was not like every other woman of her time. She was considered less than, she was mocked and derided. Devalued. But she chose to give her dreams to God anyway.

Hannah chose to place her hopes, her future, and her identity into the hands of the God who had, up to that point, not given her the life she had wanted. And when she was misjudged by Eli, the priest, she chose to continue to cry out to God despite his derision. She dared to suffer ridicule from a man of God in order to pour her heart out to God. And she did it even when it seemed that same God had forgotten her.

He had not. He simply had a different plan. A bigger plan than that of her culture's idea of what a wife and woman ought to be.

Gender Roles Are Not Enough

We know what was expected of women in Hannah's day: get married and have babies for your husband—ideally, boy babies. Motherhood gave women value in that culture. We may think our culture is more complex, and in some ways it is. Women struggling with infertility will tell you, however, that the perception of a woman's value and identity being wrapped up in the bearing of children is still pervasive in our day, and no less painful.

But there are often also other expectations placed on women, especially in Christian culture—expectations that are said to be biblical, but are they? Is this the checklist God uses to determine our value?

- ✓ A woman must keep herself looking attractive. Not too attractive, so that she's a temptation. But attractive enough to secure a husband. And then keep him from straying.
- ✓ A single woman must desire marriage.
- ✓ A married woman must desire children.
- ✓ A woman with children must not want to work outside the home. And should not. Unless her husband needs her to in order to support the family, then she must.
- ✓ A married woman must submit to her husband in all things and never contradict him. A single woman will submit to her father and other men in leadership around her.
- ✓ A woman should not have career aspirations. Her gifts and talents should be focused on service to her family, church, and community.
- ✓ A woman must consider everyone's needs before her own.
- ✓ A woman's home reflects her heart. It should always be ready to welcome others.
- ✓ A woman should be wise and intelligent, while demure and unobtrusive. Not assertive, decisive, or bold.

And this just touches on the biggest talking points in the giant tub of "shoulds" I've heard from marriage seminars and videos, women's conferences and retreats, sermons and books. I've heard them from the mouths of men about women, from women about women, from relatives and friends, from a whole host of those who believe they are spokespersons for Christ.

I've encountered the pressure of these expectations everywhere, except in the pages of my Bible. There, I find something different—not a laundry list of expectations, but a way for both men and women to become who God created them, uniquely, to be. I find a God who delights not in pressing his people into a mold, but rather in molding his people, each into a unique creation of his envisioning.

Even recently, I've heard Christians bemoaning the fact that we've become biblically illiterate and therefore don't understand the specific roles God has laid out for women. Which roles are those? Where are these roles mandated in the Bible? Where does God dictate his expectations for all women? My mind goes to Proverbs 31. Isn't that the passage that outlines the ideal woman of God?

So I turn there in my Bible, and what do I find? I find a woman of character. Trustworthy, who fears God. That's who we should all be. But that's not a role. So what does the woman in Proverbs 31 *do*? Well, she works with wool and flax. She gets up early. She considers buying a field, and she buys it. *She* buys it. She plants a vineyard. She dresses not for the pleasure of others but dresses herself in strength. Strength! This woman is not passive. She makes a profit at her businesses (she seems to have a few), and she helps the poor and needy. She does what's right and she fears the Lord. But there's no indication that she fears anything else. She makes bedcoverings for *herself* and wears fine clothes. She opens her mouth and teaches kindness with wisdom. (I notice that the text doesn't say she teaches only women and children.) And how do the people in her life respond? Not with demands, limitations, or expectations but with trust, blessing, and praise. The wisdom writer instructs all to, "Give her the fruit of her hands, and let her works praise her in the gates" (Proverbs 31:31).

Now, do I believe Proverbs 31 is asking every woman to do all these things? Must we all plant vineyards and wear purple clothes? Of course not. Rather, the description throws open the gates and showcases the fullness of what it can look like to be women who fear the Lord. We can make decisions. We can take care of our households. We can teach. We can own businesses. We can be wives and mothers. We can love and take care of others. We can reach out our hands to the needy. We can be all that God has made us to be. Here we find no narrow, restrictive roles that limit us to being of value only if we focus on satisfying a husband and raising children, or only if we fit some other predefined role for women.

There is so much we *can* do. The only thing we *must* do is fear the Lord.

Because each of us is not "just" a woman. We are each a unique creation with a God-given purpose. As I search through the Bible looking for this idea of women's roles, instead I find verses that point to the beauty and dignity of who God made us to be. I read that each of us, whether male or female, is God's masterpiece (Ephesians 2:10). We are his special work, into which he pours all the love and energy and attention to detail of a master craftsman. I read that each of us is created in Christ Jesus to do good works that God planned for us long ago. Not the same good works for all women just because they're women, but good works prepared in advance just for you, just for me. And all we must do is be obedient to the path he sets before each of us.

God has prepared works just for you to do. To settle for anything less, to be pressed into a mold by the expectations of others, is to fail to be all God has created you to be.

A Husband Is Not Enough

Hannah's story is only one of many that tells us that God has more for women, more for you and me, than our culture, perhaps especially our Christian culture, has traditionally allowed. Bible teacher Beth Moore recently stated, "We have to reckon with the fact that we—myself included—went too far. We put limitations on women that exceeded what Christ demonstrated. We did it instead of wrestling with the tension between the gospels and epistles."[1] And I would add, *without* wrestling with the tension between how we've been culturally conditioned to view women's roles versus what we see in the stories of the mighty women of the Bible.

We would do well to consider the lives of Deborah, Ruth, Lydia, Jael, and dozens of others. Of Deborah the judge and Jael the heroine, pastor and author Kelly Ladd Bishop writes, "Deborah and Jael were not neglecting their 'roles' as women or trying to become like men. They were both living into their identities as strong women and doing exactly what God called them to do! They would've failed if they'd allowed manmade boundaries to hold them back! Israel's fate at that time depended on these women being the fierce, wise, and strong leaders that they were!"[2]

Throughout the pages of the Bible, it is clear that God doesn't expect women to fit into just one traditional role. Having a perfect home isn't enough. Having children isn't enough. Having a loving husband isn't enough either.

Hannah didn't fulfill the expectations of others. And it was painful for her. She was mocked incessantly by Peninnah. She was scolded by Eli, the priest. And she was questioned by her husband, Elkanah. Why wasn't he enough for her? Even though he meant well, the question itself added yet another layer of burdensome expectation.

Elkanah's question is one we rarely consider when exploring Hannah's story. We focus instead on the pain of her infertility. We scowl at Eli's assumptions and initial criticism. But what about this idea that one's husband should be enough to satisfy?

Elkanah loved Hannah. He expected his love to quench all the longings of her heart. He believed that he should be enough to fulfill all her dreams. He wasn't. Should he have been?

The question is one women still face today. Even though we've come a long way, culture still tells us that a loving husband who provides is all a woman needs. Find Prince Charming and live happily ever after, right?

Wrong, this woman of the Bible teaches us. Elkanah was never meant to be enough to satisfy the yearnings of Hannah's heart. Nor could a child fully satisfy her either.

What she needed for her face to be "no longer sad" (1 Samuel 1:18) was the assurance that she was valued by God. Nothing else would satisfy.

Hannah was able to eat and be happy when she felt assured that God had heard her, that she mattered to the Lord of hosts. Eli the priest said to her, "Go in peace, and the God of Israel grant your petition that you have made to him" (1 Samuel 1:17). Her petition wasn't simply "give me children" or "remember me" or "remove the shame of my infertility." It was not to make her a mother just like everyone else. Rather, she asked God for something unique—a child who would be dedicated to God's service. She asked to serve God more fully, that her desires would be for the glory of God.

In her case, that meant giving birth to a son whom she wouldn't be able to raise, who would instead be dedicated to God's service at the temple. She would have to give him away. Though, later, God would give Hannah other children, three sons and two daughters (1 Samuel 2:21).

God knew who he created Hannah to be—his servant, who would become the mother of one of the greatest prophets of Israel. The love of her husband didn't—wasn't meant to—satisfy the ache within. But the reassurance that God heard her plea, and would bring about the fulfillment of who she was meant to be, cured her ache. Notice that nothing in her circumstances had yet changed when she arose from her prayer and was no longer sad. She was still childless. Peninnah was still mean-spirited. Elkanah still loved her and thought he should be enough for her. She still received a double portion at the temple. She still was not who society, culture, her rival, or even her husband thought she should be. And yet, when she aligned her will and her desires with God's purpose, her misery ended. It didn't matter what others thought because God was pleased. And he was enough.

The same is true for you. Is there anyone you're trying hard to please? What circumstances or achievements are you expecting to be "enough"? Are you seeking the approval of others instead of an encounter with the living God? Are you trying to fit someone else's mold, or are you looking to God to discover the unique woman he created you to be?

Finding Your Value

Hannah didn't pretend that Peninnah's derision wasn't painful. She also didn't pretend that a loving husband was enough to make her whole. But in her pain, there's no evidence that she ever lashed out at her rival, at her husband, or at the God who had not made her like everyone else.

Rather, we see that she simply brought her heartache to God and cried out to him. She didn't let her rival, her culture, her husband, or even a priest define her or discourage her from seeking God. Instead, she knelt before the Lord of hosts in honesty and vulnerability and placed herself in his hands.

And because she did, Hannah found her particular place in history. She found her value by seeking God and submitting to him, not by seeking to fulfill cultural norms and submitting to the expectations of others. The result was not only joy, but also a deeper understanding of the God she served. Her prayer of praise and gratitude is one of the most beautiful to be found in Scripture:

> My heart exults in the LORD;
>> my horn is exalted in the LORD. . . .
> There is none holy like the LORD:
>> for there is none besides you;
>> there is no rock like our God. . . .
> The LORD kills and brings to life;
>> he brings down to Sheol and raises up.
> The LORD makes poor and makes rich;
>> he brings low and he exalts.
> He raises up the poor from the dust;
>> he lifts the needy from the ash heap
> to make them sit with princes
>> and inherit a seat of honor.
> For the pillars of the earth are the LORD's,
>> and on them he has set the world.
>> (1 Samuel 2:1–2, 6–8)

"Horn" in Hebrew is a symbol of strength. In God alone Hannah found not only her value but her joy and strength. She found that there is nothing, no one, that can satisfy the longings of our souls as he can. In God is the power of life, a life lived in the richness of his grace. In him only is the power of lifting up, of finding meaning, of having value.

We find our worth in pursuing God himself. Not our culture's idea of who we should be, not the church's picture of what women ought to do, not even our husband's expectations of what should satisfy or make us happy.

You find your value in knowing you are God's masterpiece. He has already prepared the works for you to do. Now, you need only kneel before him, then walk in the ways he sets out for you, no matter what others may say or think, scold or expect.

Get up, eat, and, with Hannah, tell those who would devalue the person God created you to be:

> Talk no more so very proudly,
>   let not arrogance come from your mouth;
> for the LORD is a God of knowledge,
>   and by him actions are weighed.
> The bows of the mighty are broken,
>   but the feeble bind on strength.
>
> (1 Samuel 2:3–4)

These are the words of a woman who knows who she is in God. These are the words of a woman of immense value. Let them be your words as you become all God himself created you to be.

Who Is God When We're Devalued?

If you doubt, even for a moment, that you are of less value because you don't fit a mold, focus your attention on the life of Christ—the only model in Scripture that we are called to follow.

Jesus knew what it meant to not fit the expectations of others. He was not what the religious leaders thought the Messiah would or should be. He wasn't even what they believed a rabbi or a teacher should be. Over and over the religious leaders challenged and even threatened Jesus for failing to live up to their expectations.

Rabbi, why do your disciples not wash their hands? (Mark 7:5)

Rabbi, don't you know who's touching you, she's a sinful woman! (Luke 7:39)

Rabbi, don't you know it's unlawful for your disciples to pick grain on the Sabbath? (Matthew 12:2)

Rabbi, why do you eat with tax collectors and sinners? (Matthew 9:11)

Rabbi, how can you be the Messiah? You're nothing like what we think a rabbi is supposed to be. You are nothing but a criminal! (Mark 15)

And so this rabbi, God in human form, was scorned because he didn't conform to the expectations of the religious leaders of his day. Because instead of settling for people-pleasing, he chose to accomplish his purpose. He never wavered in his commitment to be who God the Father made him to be, and to pursue the purpose God had set for him. He kept his focus on his Father, not on the opinions of others. And he walked in the way determined for him.

That is who God is. Mold-breaker. Masterpiece-maker.

When we are walking in the path God sets for us, it doesn't matter how people sneer or ridicule or accuse. It only matters that we become who God created us to be. Let no one devalue you because you don't fit his or her expectations of who you ought to be, what you ought to have, or what your life should look like. Follow God. Be the woman God made you to be. Live out the unique dream he has entrusted to you. Nothing else will satisfy the longings of your soul.

Today you are You, that is truer than true.
There is no one alive who is Youer than You.

Dr. Seuss

7

ABIGAIL
Endangered

---

1 Samuel 25

The woman was discerning and beautiful, but the man was harsh and badly behaved. (1 Samuel 25:3)

Endangered. Put in peril. Exposed. We are endangered when the sin, the bad behavior, the selfishness, the meanness of another exposes us to threat. Sometimes a marriage puts a spouse in danger. Sometimes a significant other makes us vulnerable to pain and hurt. Sometimes being endangered is more a way of life than a single incident.

"We've been happily married for fifteen years." She says it with a small smile as she and her husband anticipate celebrating their thirty-fourth wedding anniversary. I do the math. Thirty-four years minus fifteen happily married years equals nineteen *un*happily married years. I remember some of those years; we've been friends that long. Those first almost-two decades nearly destroyed her. Everyone knew she shouldn't marry him. But she did anyway. She had such high hopes, such belief in love conquering all, of happily-ever-afters, before the life-dragons were truly slain. After all, he said he was a Christian. He came to church with her. He sometimes played in the church band. Surely that meant everything would be all right. Surely God would bless them and their marriage with happiness and joy.

But at parties, he drank too much. Sometimes he smoked pot. He spent money on gadgets when there wasn't enough to buy groceries. And none of that changed after marriage.

But something else changed.

After marriage, the compliments slowly faded away. The declarations of love became fewer and fewer. And the criticism began. He called her stupid. He blamed her for all the things that were wrong in their lives. Every argument left her feeling worthless and in despair as he projected his faults onto her and she bore the weight of them.

The disparaging way he spoke to her kept her down, defeated, miserable for nineteen long years. I remember the lunches where she spilled out her pain and hopelessness. She hated her life. She was afraid to leave, afraid to stay. But as a young mother with no college degree, no marketable skills, and lots of self-doubt, she believed she was stuck. Or at least, he had convinced her that he was her only option.

She made mistakes too. Depression led to a secret addiction to pills, which led to an affair, which led to more depression and more contemptuous comments from her husband.

But her marriage didn't end at nineteen years. It's been thirty-four. And the last fifteen have been markedly different. Not every moment has been bliss, but she's been happy. They've been happy. And it didn't happen because her husband woke up one day and decided to change. It happened because she did. She decided to do right and to choose wisely, no matter what he did. No matter if he was harsh, foolishness, or hurtful.

She would do right. And that allowed God to accomplish things in her life she could never have accomplished on her own. For my friend, it meant a new era in her marriage that eventually led to healing and happiness. However, it won't mean that for everyone stuck in an oppressive relationship.

It didn't mean that for Abigail, the wife of Nabal, whose name means "fool" in Hebrew. And yet, she is a heroine, praised by the biblical writer who commends her intelligence and good judgment. I wonder what hope she might offer to women today who feel trapped in a repressive relationship, who have given up or are about to because they feel like there isn't anything they can do to change their situation.

What wisdom would she give if she told her story to women living three thousand years later? Perhaps she would say something like this . . .

ABIGAIL SPEAKS OUT

I would have expected my husband to at least be respectful of David. After all, the prophet Samuel, who had just died and been mourned by all Israel, had anointed David king. King Saul hadn't yet acknowledged it, but we all knew. David was a hero. He was favored by our God. He was not a man to be trifled with.

And he asked us for so little. He sent ten young men to say to my husband, "Peace be to you, and peace be to your house, and peace be to all that you have." A greeting of friendship, of kindness, of respect. And there was more.

"I hear that you have shearers. Now your shepherds have been with us, and we did them no harm, and they missed nothing all the time they were in Carmel." His men had protected our sheep and shepherds, as a courtesy, a kindness, when his men could have taken what they wanted by force. But instead of taking, they had given. They had protected our men and sheep, and that was before we had done a thing for David.

The message continued. "Ask your young men, and they will tell you. Therefore let my young men find favor in your eyes, for we come on a feast day. Please give whatever you have at hand to your servants and to your son David."

A simple request. Easily fulfilled. He wasn't asking more than we could give. We had enough, and more. My husband had three thousand sheep and one thousand goats! Even a lavish feast for David and his men would barely make a dent in our riches. God had blessed us with plenty, and plenty more to share with his anointed king.

But my husband, Nabal, wasn't known for his generosity. So I waited. I prayed. I chewed my lip and wondered what answer my husband would give. He was not a wise man. He was not kind. Not to me, not to others. In our region, he was known to be harsh and badly behaved. And they didn't even know what happened behind closed doors, when it was just me and the servants. When we were alone.

And I was supposed to just listen, endure, submit. A man may wear a mask of righteousness in public, but his family knows the truth. His wife knows. And my husband didn't even bother with a well-mannered persona in public. Everyone could see what kind of man he was.

I waited in the kitchen, waited for word of my husband's foolishness, though I hoped for better. Surely, he wouldn't endanger us all. Certainly, he would send a gift to David. David was a mighty warrior who led mighty men. My husband would remember that when he made his reply. At least, I hoped so.

It was a vain hope.

Later, a young man, one of the shearers, came bursting into the room. "Behold," he panted, "David sent messengers out of the wilderness to greet our master, and he railed at them."

Oh no! No, no, no!

"The men were very good to us, and we suffered no harm, and we did not miss anything when we were in the fields, as long as we went with them. They were a wall to us both by night and by day, all the while we were with them keeping the sheep."

I heard the words, and I cringed. My breath stopped.

The young man must have come straight to me when he heard. And he must have run. He looked at me, his gaze desperate. "Now therefore know this and consider what you should do, for harm is determined against our master and against all his house, and he is such a worthless man that one cannot speak to him."

I rubbed my hand over my face. To choose to give was the man's duty. He was to show hospitality. To refuse to do so . . .

I shuddered. It was unthinkable. His greed, his pride, would be the death of him, and of us all.

There was no way out. I couldn't leave. The servants would all be sacrificed. I couldn't hide. And I surely couldn't convince Nabal to change his mind. No one could do that.

He had chosen to refuse David and bring doom on us all.

I could choose to obey my husband, follow his wishes. Submit to his folly. Or I could dare to do what was right, whether or not Nabal would shame me, blame me, hate me. Whether or not David would kill me.

I rushed to gather two hundred loaves and two skins of our best wine. I added five seahs of parched grain and five sheep already prepared. Then, I called for one hundred clusters of raisins and two hundred cakes of figs. We laid all the food on donkeys and then I sent my young men ahead. "Go on before me," I told them. "Behold, I come after you."

But I did not tell my husband.

Did I do wrong? Should I have submitted to his foolishness? Should I have deferred to him, knowing it meant our doom? Would God pardon me if I embraced folly just because I am married to a fool? No, my God asks more of me than that. He asks me, even me, a woman, to live in righteousness, to follow his wisdom and his ways above any other.

Under cover of the mountain, I rode my donkey toward David's camp. Then I saw the shadows moving toward me. David and his men. They came down.

I swallowed hard, stopped my donkey, and quickly dismounted. When David approached me, I fell before him, on my face, bowed to the ground at his feet. "On me alone, my lord, be the guilt. Please let your servant speak in your ears, and hear the words of your servant." I waited. Would he listen to me, a woman and a wife acting outside her husband's authority? Would he heed my plea?

"Let not my lord regard this worthless fellow, Nabal, for as his name is, so is he. Nabal is his name, and folly is with him." I swallowed. They were harsh words, but David did not rebuke me. He simply waited for me to continue.

I drew a deep breath. "But I your servant did not see the young men of my lord, whom you sent. Now then, my lord, as the Lord lives, and as your soul lives, because the Lord has restrained you from bloodguilt and from saving with your own hand, now then let your enemies and those who seek to do evil to my lord be as Nabal. And now let this present that your servant has brought to my lord be given to the young men who follow my lord."

I paused. Would he hear the truth as I made no excuses for my husband, and yet still pleaded for his life? Begged the king to spare a fool and keep his own hands free of bloodguilt?

"Please forgive the trespass of your servant," I continued. "For the Lord will certainly make my lord a sure house, because my lord is fighting the battles of the Lord, and evil shall not be found in you so long as you live." I waited, the smell of dust in my nostrils, but David said nothing.

I glanced up enough to look at his sandals, my voice growing steady as God put words of blessing into my mouth for his anointed king. "If men rise up to pursue you and to seek your life, the life of my lord shall be bound in the bundle of the living in the care of the Lord your God. And the lives of your enemies he shall sling out as from the hollow of a sling."

Then I took courage to deliver my final argument, my final plea. "And when the Lord has done to my lord according to all the good that he has spoken concerning you and has appointed you prince over Israel, my lord shall have no cause of grief or pangs of conscience for having shed blood without cause or for my lord working salvation himself. And when the Lord has dealt well with my lord, then remember your servant."

I dared to glance up. Would he be angry? Would he smite me for daring to give advice to so mighty a man?

But no, he was almost, almost . . . smiling?

He motioned for me to rise.

"Blessed be the Lord, the God of Israel, who sent you this day to meet me! Blessed be your discretion, and blessed be you, who have kept me this day from bloodguilt and from working salvation with my own hand! For as surely as the Lord, the God of Israel, lives, who has restrained me from hurting you, unless you had hurried and come to meet me, truly by morning there had not been left to Nabal so much as one male."

He asked his men to receive the gifts of food that I'd brought. "Go up in peace to your house," he said. "See, I have obeyed your voice, and I have granted your petition."

The anointed king had obeyed *my* voice. He had listened to me. And so he had chosen to spare Nabal, despite my husband's foolishness. In doing so, he spared us all. He had even praised me for bringing to him the wisdom of our God. I had done what was right. I had been faithful first to my God and his.

Now I had to go back to my husband to tell him what I had done. Righteousness is not without risk.

When I returned home, there was a great feast underway, a feast fit for a king! He who could not spare a dozen loaves for the anointed and future king of Israel could waste a king-sized feast on himself and his friends. I found my husband at the main table, laughing and shouting, drunk. Very drunk.

There was no use speaking to him now. I turned and left. I waited until morning.

When the wine had gone out of my husband, I told him what I had done. I told him what I'd given to David, what I'd said, and what David had said in return.

I waited for his anger. I waited for shouting, shame, a slap across my face. But nothing ever came. Instead, my husband clutched his chest, gasped, and became like stone.

I gasped too. And called for the servants.

Nabal never moved again. Ten days later, he died in his bed.

I didn't have to tell him he was a fool. I didn't have to scold him, correct him, or try to force him to be the man he should have been. But neither did I blindly obey him. I wasn't powerless. I had only to do what was right and wise in the eyes of God. And God took care of the rest.

When David heard of my husband's death, he sent a message asking me to become his wife, to become a queen in Israel. Both the king and our God had honored me.

Endangered

So what do you do when you're married to a man whose choices are a danger to you? What if he drinks too much, takes drugs, gambles, or has a mean streak? What if he's generally a good guy but sometimes selfish, impulsive, or unwise? What do you do when you're told that God wants you to submit and your role is to obey your husband, regardless of his poor judgment or instability?

In Christian circles, we hear a lot about submission in marriage. Many of us have been told over and over that it is the duty of a wife to acquiesce to her husband's leadership. The words of the apostle Paul—that wives submit to their husbands because the husband is head of the wife as Christ is head of the church—are often quoted (Ephesians 5:22–24). Though just as often, the admonition that precedes these words—to submit to *one another* out of reverence to Christ—are left out (Ephesians 5:21).

To be godly, we are told, is to yield to men—to husbands and to bosses, to coaches and to fathers, to pastors and to uncles, and to every other man in our lives. Even when those men are bullies. Even when those men are as stubborn and selfish, as reckless and cruel as Nabal.

Well, that doesn't make good sense. Yet the Bible clearly tells us to submit to our husbands. So, should we do so only when they are perfect? That doesn't make sense either. It would essentially make the concept of submission meaningless. No man, no human being, is perfect.

So, what's the answer?

What if the truth lies not in the question of whether or not to submit, but rather in the very definition of submission itself? What if we've misunderstood the concept of submission?

Does it mean to obey?

Does it mean to defer in all decisions?

Does it mean to follow a husband's poor choices and dangerous decrees?

Does it mean a husband always has the final say?

Perhaps it's time to examine our definition of submission through a careful consideration of the story of Abigail and Nabal.

Every mention of Abigail in 1 Samuel is positive and affirming. Besides "beautiful," the text describes her as "discerning" (25:3). Other translations use the words "sensible" or "intelligent." David says to her, "Blessed be your discretion, and blessed be you" (v. 33). At no point is she rebuked for failing to submit to her husband. In fact, just the opposite is true—she is commended.

So, let's allow Abigail to be our guide. Let's see what she does, what she doesn't do, and what submission looks like in the life of this woman who was highly praised.

We begin by considering what submission is not.

What Abigail Didn't Do

Abigail was married to a fool. The Bible describes the couple this way: "The woman was discerning and beautiful, but the man was harsh and badly behaved" (1 Samuel 25:3). Nabal's demeanor and dark character not only would have made Abigail's life miserable, they also endangered her and others in the household.

When she discovered that her husband had refused David's request and insulted the anointed king, she took immediate and decisive action to correct the folly. What she didn't do, however, is provoke Nabal. She didn't take it upon herself to point out all his character flaws, all his mistakes, all his poor choices. She didn't tell him he was wrong or that she was smarter than he was. She didn't yell at him, scorn him, shame him. In fact, she didn't focus on him and his faults at all. Ponder that for a moment.

There may well come a time in our lives when we need to confront our Nabals. We may need to speak up. And yet, we never need to speak with derision. We don't need to go out of our way to hurt and harm with our words. In the process of confronting, we don't need to adopt the other person's foolishness and make it our own. If we must confront in order to bring about righteousness, then we must do it righteously. With thoughtfulness and respect. In Abigail's case, a confrontation was not likely to result in positive change. She was able to discern that and act wisely because she allowed room for reason despite fearful, unfair circumstances.

Abigail didn't waste time railing at Nabal. She didn't fret. She didn't bemoan her fate. She didn't get all tied up in a knot, even though she knew full well the seriousness of Nabal's offense and the probable outcome—death for them all. Nor did she try to be God to her husband, to fix him, to force him to much-needed repentance. Instead, she followed the submission ideal embodied by Sarah, which the apostle Peter wrote about centuries later: "For this is how the holy women who hoped in God used to adorn themselves, by submitting to their own husbands, as Sarah obeyed Abraham, calling him lord. And you are her children, if you do good and do not fear anything that is frightening" (1 Peter 3:5–6).

Reread that last line one more time. Peter stresses two things for holy women.

Do good.

Don't be afraid.

That's what submission is: Do good; don't be afraid.

To do that, to truly "submit" we must be like Abigail, who didn't waste a moment of time, thought, energy, effort, angst, anger, fear, frustration on the faults of her husband. Her simple decision not to be consumed by what was wrong with Nabal allowed her to focus all of her efforts on taking proper action—on doing good.

Abigail did not obsess over her husband's wrongdoing.

But neither did she comply with his foolishness. He clearly chose to give nothing to David and doubled down on his decision with stinging insults. Yet, despite her husband's decision, Abigail quickly went against it, and not just by a little. She gathered not a few meager leftovers as a token gift for David, but rather two hundred loaves of bread, two full skins of wine, five sheep, five seahs of grain, one hundred clusters of raisins, and two hundred cakes of figs. She was lavish in her defiance of her husband's expressed wishes!

So what does her example mean? It demonstrates that submission does not mean accepting abuse, foolishness, harsh treatment, or going along with dangerous decisions and behaviors. It does not mean—it never means—we have to silently endure the sin done to us or to those around us. We do not need to comply with sinful behavior!

That's not what Abigail did, and she was highly acclaimed. So, what else is submission *not*?

To answer that question, let's look more closely at the interaction between Abigail and David. When David approached her, Abigail could easily have advocated for the survival of herself and her household alone. She could have urged David to take vengeance only on Nabal. She could have gotten David to free her from her foolish husband and goaded him to take his revenge and hers.

Instead, she begged for mercy, not only for herself and her household, but for Nabal as well. And in pleading for Nabal, she also pleaded for David's integrity. She didn't seek revenge. She didn't attempt to get back at a foolish husband for his harsh and dangerous ways. She stayed David's hand, to save a man who didn't deserve it, didn't want help, refused to repent or recognize wisdom. And she kept David from making a rash decision of his own.

At the same time, Abigail didn't make excuses for her husband. She told the truth. "Nabal is his name, and folly is with him," she said (1 Samuel 25:25). In both her actions and her appeal to David, she acknowledged the sin of her spouse. There was no minimizing or rationalizing. No, "Oh, he isn't that bad, he just had a tough day." Submission isn't making excuses for bad behavior.

Abigail submitted to her relationship with a fool by *not* allowing her fears of what might happen to force her into doing whatever he wanted, by *not* capitulating to his demands and folly, by *not* blindly obeying. She submitted by courageously doing good, by acting wisely, by allowing God to deal with her husband as God saw fit.

So, among other things, this is what biblical submission isn't:

- Supporting sin
- Passively accepting another's direction
- Making excuses
- Agreeing to foolishness because a husband, boss, or other man insists on it

Nor does biblical submission allow for trying to be God in a man's life by correcting, scolding, punishing, or scheming for dominance or control. So what is biblical submission? To find out, let's consider what Abigail did do.

What Abigail Did Do

First, before anything had even happened, Abigail was ready to take action. She kept herself informed about what God was doing in her nation. She knew who David was, and how God was moving in Israel (1 Samuel 25:28–30). Although Nabal insulted David, Abigail knew that the Lord had chosen David to be the king of Israel. She knew David had fought the Lord's battles and that God was for him. She also knew what God had promised to David. She didn't depend on her husband's learning and knowledge—who seemed not to know, or at least not to care, about who David was. Because of her knowledge, she was ready when she needed to make quick decisions and take action.

Furthermore, it was her habit to pursue righteousness. Her defining characteristics were discernment and discretion (1 Samuel 25:3, 33). She practiced wisdom routinely, so when a need arose, the young men knew who they could turn to. They trusted her ability to act both wisely and swiftly in a crisis. The daily practice of wisdom and discernment, rather than blindly following her husband's lead, allowed her to intervene and save not only her own life, but also the lives of her household, and of her foolish husband.

She did what was right and what was wise, no matter what. She used everything in her power for righteousness, for blessing others, for protecting those given to her to protect— her servants, her husband, and even David, her future king. Instead of bemoaning her fate, she took action. She saw what needed to be done and she did it. No excuses.

She let God deal with Nabal. And she urged David to do the same.

In doing so, she demonstrated the heart of true submission. She submitted to David, not so much by throwing herself at his feet, but rather by doing and advising what was best for David. She submitted to her husband in the same way. She did what was best for Nabal, despite his reckless decision to endanger them all.

That's the heart of biblical submission—doing what is best for the other. Submission is not synonymous with obedience, but rather a partner to righteousness, wisdom, and love.

Abigail, who had likely suffered the most at the hands of Nabal, was the voice of righteousness for him, her household, and even for David, the anointed king.

You too can be the voice for righteousness, wisdom, and love. You can choose to do what's right and to speak what's right. You can advise your children, your friends, your coworkers, not based on the foolishness of whomever the Nabal in your life might be, but on the constancy of Christ.

He has called you to do good, and not to fear what is frightening. To speak and act wisely and leave the rest to God.

When you need guidance, ask for it. Here is the promise and counsel of Scripture:

> If you need wisdom, ask our generous God, and he will give it to you. He will not rebuke you for asking. But when you ask him, be sure that your faith is in God alone. Do not waver, for a person with divided loyalty is as unsettled as a wave of the sea that is blown and tossed by the wind. (James 1:5–6 NLT)

We need to focus on following God, doing right, and not splitting our loyalty between God and our Nabal. We cannot try to accommodate or appease the other person's foolishness and flaws while asking for wisdom for ourselves. Instead, we embrace the call of Scripture to set our sights on the prize of steadfast faith:

> Let us run with endurance the race that is set before us, looking to Jesus, the founder and perfecter of our faith, who for the joy that was set before him endured the cross, despising the shame, and is seated at the right hand of the throne of God. (Hebrews 12:1–2)

For the joy set before us, we, like Abigail, focus on whatever it is we can do to make things right—for ourselves and for those within our sphere of care.

For the joy set before us, we turn away from revenge and derision so that we may turn toward Christ and his righteousness and love.

For the joy set before us, we give our undivided loyalty to Christ and submit our lives to him.

The Truth about Submission

So what's the bottom line about this controversial subject of women's submission? So often we are told it means the man is always in control. Men lead. Women follow. We quote the words of the apostle Paul, "For the husband is the head of the wife even as Christ is the head of the church, his body, and is himself its Savior" (Ephesians 5:23), and conclude it means that a wife must obey everything a man says, no matter what, just as the church should obey Christ in everything.

But every verse of Scripture must be interpreted in light of the whole witness of the Bible, not just a verse or two plucked out and applied without regard for the rest. If God intended women to submit to the point of going along with foolishness and folly, then Abigail would have been rebuked. The Proverbs 31 woman would be described much different. And stories such as those of Deborah and Jael would contain condemnation instead of commendation.

The basis for the kind of submission laid out by both the Old and New Testaments is wisdom and righteousness. Submission is not to be a jockeying for position, to be above or to be below. Rather, as the apostle Paul says, we are to "submit to one another out of reverence for Christ" (Ephesians 5:21 NIV). We listen, we heed, we value the other person. We consider his needs as well as our own. But when his decisions are sinful, dangerous, or foolish, we cannot and should not follow. Submitting means submitting to wisdom, submitting to what's right, submitting to God and his will above all.

And yet, too often we hold back from doing what's right because we're afraid. We might even use submission as an excuse to accommodate sin because it can be risky to stand up and do the right thing. We might be blamed. We might be shamed. We might even suffer additional abuse. But if we are to have an undivided loyalty to God, we have to risk submitting to him—to do what is wise and right even when it conflicts with what a husband or any other human being expects.

Who Is God When We're Endangered?

Just like Abigail, we submit to God. But we don't do it alone. We don't do it through grit and determination. We don't do it through clenched teeth because "that book we're reading" says we have to.

Rather, we do it in the power of a God who gives us what we need. God is Spirit. And the Spirit develops in us the fruit we need to submit in the right way, even when it's difficult. The Spirit empowers us, as it did Abigail, to do good and not succumb to fear.

Each fruit of the Spirit (Galatians 5:22–23) illuminates submission in its fullness. We see it in Abigail's life. Her words and actions demonstrate that the fruit of authentic submission is characterized by love, joy, peace, patience, kindness, goodness, faithfulness, gentleness, and self-control.

Consider how closely the fruits of the Spirit match the heart of submission so that you can know God is with you, giving you whatever you need to be the woman he has called you to be.

Love. In hope and faith, we can put the needs and well-being of others first.

Joy. For the joy set before us, we can endure, looking to Jesus for our strength and hope.

Peace. We can choose to focus on God and his faithfulness rather than the flaws and foolishness of our Nabal. We can encounter the Nabal in our lives with peace and reason rather than with angst and agitation.

Patience. We can let God take care of the outcomes and the timing. We can rest without needing to fix our husband, our boss, our father, or any other man in our life. We can cooperate with God by making wise decisions and taking wise actions. Then we can watch and wait as God moves.

Kindness. We can choose to be kind. Mean-spirited retaliation isn't God's way. We don't have to give in to foolishness, but neither do we have to respond to our Nabal in a Nabal-like way. We can pursue the righteousness of God for the benefit of all, even the very one who is being unkind.

Goodness. We can do right no matter what, even when it's scary. Even when it's risky. We can refuse to use "submission" as an excuse to go along with the sin or foolishness of our Nabal. We can do good.

Faithfulness. We can refuse to let anyone cause us to sin. We can be faithful to God's call in our lives. A Nabal may be terrible, abusive, "harsh and badly behaved," but we don't have to give him the power to destroy us by pushing us into sin. We can be loyal to Christ. We can hold fast to our integrity, not letting our Nabal destroy our faith—and if we already have allowed that, we can repent. Then we can make a different choice. Faithfulness can start today. Right now. One wise word, one courageous action at a time.

Gentleness. We can walk in gentleness instead of passivity. We can choose to not just let whatever happens happen, without care or prayer. Rather, we can walk in the ways of God, especially when everything in us wants to walk in the ways of either apathy or anger and retaliation—to give up and give in or to yell back, accuse, condemn, spew words of hate, and take revenge. Instead, we can gently pursue God's will in all areas of our lives.

Self-control. We can choose self-control over self-seeking. We can practice the discipline of doing right so we don't give in to the impulse of getting back at Nabal or cringing away in fear. Self-control empowers us to seek God, and to remember who we are. We are beloved children. We are daughters of the King. We are the bride of Christ.

When you are surrounded by the foolishness or threats of your Nabal, remember the wisdom and discretion of Abigail. Remember the fruits of the Spirit. And remember who you are in God. You are precious. You are loved. You are confident. You can be faithful and gentle and good and kind. You belong to the God of the universe, your Creator, and he loves you.

And when you forget, when you fail, don't despair. Our God is a forgiving God who lavishes his gifts with abundance. He is the master farmer who can grow the fruits of the Spirit in you so that your life produces a bountiful harvest. So even when we fail or lose faith, we are not without hope. We can ask forgiveness. We can start over.

So start today with a new vision of submission, a vision that requires courage to do right no matter how fearful, frustrated, angry, hurt, betrayed you feel. Choose to practice wisdom and kindness. Gather the loaves and wine, sheep, grain, and clusters of raisins, cakes of figs, gather everything you have—your hopes, your dreams, your fears, your weaknesses, your strengths, your successes and failures. Take them all to the King of Kings. Lay them at his feet. Make no excuses. Whisper no lies. Ask simply that he remember you.

And so be filled with the fruits of the Spirit.

Because that's what true submission looks like. And that's the beauty and wonder of what God longs to do in you, for you, with you.

Submit to him.

You may encounter many defeats, but you must not be defeated. In fact, it may be necessary to encounter the defeats, so you can know who you are, what you rise from, how you can still come out of it.

Maya Angelou

8

BATHSHEBA

Sexualized

---

2 Samuel 11–12

It happened, late one afternoon, when David arose from his couch and was walking on the roof of the king's house, that he saw from the roof a woman bathing; and the woman was very beautiful. (2 Samuel 11:2)

Sexualized. According to the American Psychological Association, that's what happens when a woman is "made into a thing for others' sexual use, rather than seen as a person with the capacity for independent action and decision making."[1] It's when a woman's value is derived or perceived to derive solely from her sexual appeal to a man. Only outward beauty matters. Only the lust of another counts.

Influential men. Sexualized, objectified women. It's an all too common story.

———— ◦ ◦ ◦ ————

On October 5, 2017, the *New York Times* published a bomb-shell article on Hollywood film producer Harvey Weinstein, detailing allegations of sexual harassment and rape spanning decades.[2] One year later, the paper published another article outlining the cases of 201 other powerful, high-profile men who had subsequently lost jobs or major roles after being accused of sexual misconduct in the workplace.[3] Two-hundred-one! From media directors and producers to editors and writers. From federal and state legislators to business and nonprofit executives. Photographers, professors, principals, and . . . pastors.

What do we do when we're sexualized, viewed only as an object to satisfy someone else's sexual pleasure, to be taken at a whim, to be acquired like property? How do we maintain dignity, faith, and hope when our very humanity is threatened because an influential man objectified us for lust? How do we protect ourselves when a man targets us, breaks laws to satisfy his own desires, and manipulates us and others just because he thinks he's entitled or somehow powerful enough to be above the law?

Bathsheba is a woman who suffered all these things and more. She was targeted and used by a powerful king, who subsequently had her husband murdered so he could marry her as cover for his sin and her pregnancy. Then, as a consequence for his crimes, her infant son died. What might she say to us about these things if she could speak today? Perhaps through her story, we will find a fierce redemption beyond sexualization and staggering loss. Perhaps we will find a God who both sees and redeems, especially those who have suffered tragic injustices . . .

BATHSHEBA SPEAKS OUT

It was the spring of the year, when kings go out to battle. My story always starts there, in the spring, when the air was cool, the grasses green, the flowers of the fields in bloom outside the city.

Some say the season doesn't matter. But it matters to me. You remember everything about the day when your life changed forever.

And that day, it was spring. And King David should have been on a battlefield.

He wasn't.

Late one afternoon, just after my time of the month had come to an end, I climbed to the roof of our home for a bath to wash away my uncleanness. Just as I did every month. Just as every woman did. The roof was high. No surrounding building except the king's palace was high enough for anyone to see me. It shouldn't have mattered. After all, it was spring. It was the time when kings went off to war.

I bathed, I dressed, I went inside. A short time later, a knock came at my door. I frowned. No one should be knocking now. My husband, Uriah, one of David's mighty men, was gone with the armies. I was alone.

I hesitated, then walked toward the door. It opened before I reached it. Men stood outside. Messengers of the king.

What could the king want from me? He didn't even know me. Perhaps there was news of my husband? But why would I have to be brought to the king?

I stepped back.

But you don't say no to a king.

It didn't matter why he summoned me. It didn't matter what I thought, what I wanted, what I had to say.

The messengers took me to the king.

He told me I was beautiful. He told me I made his heart race. He said that all he wanted was me. And he took me, like a possession, like a thing to be stolen and used.

Not like a person with feelings, dreams, desires—or a husband of her own.

Then he sent me back to my house. As if nothing happened. As if there were no sin, and would be no consequences.

A month passed, and a little more. My monthly uncleanness didn't come. I was sick, bloated. Pregnant.

I sent word to the king. I would not be stoned as a wanton woman when it was the king himself who took me and lay with me. A man of power, and I only the wife of a warrior. A woman and not a king.

I waited.

And heard nothing.

One day not long after, my neighbor came to me in the afternoon. She told me Uriah was back from the battlefield. The king had called him home. How wonderful, she said, that he was being honored. The king must value him specially.

But I knew the truth.

David had called Uriah home to cover his sin. To make my husband lie with me so the child would be seen as his.

But he didn't know Uriah as I did. Uriah would not come home. He would not lie with me when his men were still on the battlefield. Uriah was a righteous man. I was blessed to be his wife.

As expected, Uriah did not come home. He slept at the door of the king's house with all the servants. He stayed three days, but he never came home. Then, he returned to battle, and I never saw him again.

Word came that he died on the battlefield. Struck down. Lost to the enemy.

So convenient for David. But it broke my heart.

David stole from me the purity of my marriage bed. He took from me what was never his. And then he arranged for the death of my husband, a man more righteous than himself.

I thought I had lost everything, but there was more to lose.

After my husband's death, David took me into his household and made me his wife. A prophet told David that our child, the child of his sin and my shame, would die. And he did. I lost my firstborn son.

But God did not forget me. He redeemed my loss. He remembered my pain.

I had another son, and he became king after his father. All of Israel flourished under his rule. David called his name Solomon, but Nathan the prophet called him by another name, a name of blessing. And so did I.

I called him Jedidiah, which means beloved of the Lord. My son was beloved of God.

And despite all that happened to me, so was I.

Sexualized

David didn't know who Bathsheba was when he first saw and desired her. He didn't know her name, her identity, her family situation, her character, or anything about her. All he knew was that he wanted her. Her value in his eyes came solely from her sexual appeal. He viewed her as a sexual object, not as a human being loved and created uniquely by God.

Lost in the way the story is told is the likelihood that Bathsheba may have had desires of her own, or hopes and dreams for her own future. She had married a righteous man who was highly regarded as one of King David's mighty men (2 Samuel 23:8–39). Her position was secure. According to Nathan the prophet, her husband loved her and cared for her (2 Samuel 12). She probably dreamed of having children and a big family once her husband came back from the battle-field. She would establish her home and her future with a man she loved.

But all that changed when another man, a powerful man, happened to be wandering around his rooftop and neglecting his duties as king. King David had forgotten that his position of power was a position of service to his people. Instead, he used his power to serve himself, to feed his lust and indulge his sexual pleasure. He was king and felt entitled to whatever he wanted. And what he wanted was the body of the woman he saw bathing on another man's rooftop.

For Man's Pleasure?

Sometimes those in positions of authority use the power of their position to satisfy their own sinful desires. They forget the principle made popular in our time by Spider-Man's motto, "With great power comes great responsibility," or as Luke 12:48 (NIV) puts it, "From everyone who has been given much, much will be demanded; and from the one who has been entrusted with much, much more will be asked." Every truly great leader remembers and lives by this principle. Leaders have power so they can serve and protect those for whom they are responsible. Positions of authority—parent, teacher, boss, coach—are positions of service.

But in our culture, as well as Bathsheba's, some have used their authority not to serve but to abuse. They believe the law or the rules that apply to other people somehow don't apply to them. They are above all that. They believe they have the right to do whatever they want to whomever they want. And sometimes what these powerful men want is not to partner with women for the good of all, but to use women to satisfy their own sexual desires. To feed their own out-of-control lust.

A story came out a few years ago about a powerful man who systematically and repeatedly abused the girls in his care. The man was Larry Nassar, former USA Gymnastics national team doctor and osteopathic physician at Michigan State University. Rachael Denhollander, a former gymnast, was among the first to speak publicly about Nassar's serial abuse. Nassar was ultimately sentenced for first-degree sexual conduct involving more than 160 young women and girls, some as young as six. But the number of women who have come forward is well over 300.

Compared to Nassar, David's sin seems much less severe. After all, Bathsheba was just one grown and married woman, not hundreds of underage girls. And yet, at the root of both stories we find the same warped sexualization of women. We find a man with power and influence using that power to make a girl, or a woman, into a thing for his own sexual use.

When men sexualize women in this way, when they objectify them by indulging a fantasy in which women exist solely for their own pleasure, they dehumanize women. And what happens next is always ugly. For the gymnasts, that dehumanization resulted in serial sexual abuse of girls whose bodies were supposed to be receiving medical care that would result in better gymnastics performance, not the satisfaction of a man's sexual cravings. Nassar had a job to do—to serve the girls on the gymnastics team. He served himself instead. David had a job too, to protect the subjects of his kingdom. But he wasn't doing that. And for Bathsheba, David's failure to be a good leader led to forced adultery, the death of her husband, and the loss of her firstborn son. For others, sexualization has been the precursor to rape, sexual harassment, loss of jobs and opportunities, unwanted sexual advances, inappropriate touch, and a host of other violations.

Sexualization is not an issue to be shrugged off with, "Oh, men are just that way. Boys will be boys, after all." No, this sort of sexual objectification is a poison that corrupts a man's soul and endangers the women around him.

Why? Because sexualization goes against the very fabric of who God created men and women to be—corresponding partners of equal value, significance, and worth in the eyes of God and in his creation.

God never intended a woman's worth to be tied to a man's lust.

Worth and Want

So, what do we learn about this plague of sexualization from David's lust for Bathsheba? First, we learn that sexualization is not the fault of women who are so tempting and seductive that the poor men just can't help themselves.

The biblical text does not support the idea that it was Bathsheba's seductive ways that caused David to sin. Yet, over the years, she has often been misrepresented as a seductress by both theologians and pop culture. The 1985 movie *King David* shows her seductively bathing her bare breasts, suggesting that David, upon seeing her, could not help himself. Many argue that she must have been at least partially to blame and therefore complicit in David's sin. "There is little doubt that this woman . . . acted immodestly," writes David Guzik in the *Enduring Word Bible Commentary*. "*Certainly* she knew that her bath was visible from the roof of the palace."[4] Guzik goes on to quote Carl Friedrich Keil and Franz Delitzsch whose *Commentary on the Old Testament* makes a common assertion that "there is no intimation whatever that David brought Bathsheba into his palace through craft or violence, but rather that she came at his request without any hesitation, and offered no resistance to his desires. Consequently Bathsheba is not to be regarded as free from blame." Various preachers and writers have suggested that Bathsheba shouldn't have been bathing where she was, or even that she was actually trying to seduce the king by bathing where she knew he could see her. Some have suggested that she was lonely or enamored by the idea of a relationship with a powerful king. *Nonsense!*

What evidence can we find for these often-accepted and often-unquestioned portrayals of this woman in Scripture? After careful search, we find there is nothing—*nothing*—in the text to support such notions. Scripture clearly states that Bathsheba was doing what all women in that culture did— she was bathing to clean herself after her monthly period. Washing afterward was not only a practical necessity but also a ritualistic requirement so that she would be considered "clean" again and able to participate in the social and religious life of her community. There is no suggestion in the text that her motives were to seduce, tempt, or ensnare a king or anyone else. The only motive mentioned in the text is "purifying herself"—an indication that she was acting righteously, according to the law.

As for the assertion that she didn't object to David's desire to sleep with her, did she know why the king was summoning her? Could she have defied a king? The text is very sparse. In a single verse, 2 Samuel 11:4, the Bible tells of the whole act: "So David sent messengers and took her, and she came to him, and he lay with her. . . . Then she returned to her house." David was the one in power. Bathsheba was not. He wanted to have sex with her. So he did.

Interpretations of Bathsheba's story that wander far from what the Bible text supplies—that set her up as power-hungry temptress—demonstrate that too often people assume that if a powerful man lusts after a woman she must have done something to entice him. Her skirt was too short, her neckline too low, her perfume too strong. She gave him "signs," or smiled too much, or walked a certain way, or laughed at his jokes, or let a little skin show on her shoulder, belly, or back.

Recently, one of my very conservatively dressed daughters was chastised by a staff member at her Christian high school because a slip of skin on her back showed when she leaned over to pick up her napkin from the floor at lunchtime. That bit of uncovered flesh might distract the boys. *Really?* What are we communicating to our young women when we place the blame for boys' lust on an inadvertent sliver of a young woman's skin?

The truth is, the Bible does not support the idea that a man's sexual sin can be blamed on his victim. And nowhere in the story of Bathsheba and King David is there even a hint that Bathsheba is to blame for David's lust, for his fornication, or for the murder of her husband. She was not even chastised for adultery. Instead, she was likened to an innocent little ewe lamb.

It is David alone whom the prophet Nathan harshly rebuked and on whom he pronounced severe consequences from God. David was held responsible. David was rebuked. David was disciplined.

Bathsheba, however, was not condemned, though she did suffer consequences. At David's hands, because of his sin, she lost everything: her purity and fidelity to her husband, her husband himself, her home, and her firstborn son. But God didn't leave her bereft. He redeemed her losses with an extraordinary purpose. Of all David's wives, it was she who birthed and raised Solomon, who later became king and ushered in the golden age of Israel. God saw her as valuable and precious and gave her a noble place in her nation's history. He honored her in a way she could accept and embrace. In God's economy, she became more than an object for a man's sexual pleasure. She became one of the women whose stories are woven into the lineage of Christ. God did that. Not David. God. Because he loved her.

Who Is God When We're Sexualized?

God did not see Bathsheba's value in terms of her sexual desirability. After all, in the words of the prophet Nathan, she was likened to a little ewe lamb. Let's revisit that image. It conveys the idea of a sweet and innocent lamb who was loved and cherished. The lamb was even described as being "like a daughter." A baby sheep is not a sexual image. Yet that is the image God ascribes to Bathsheba through the words of his prophet.

To David, it was Bathsheba's sexual desirability that mattered. To God, what mattered most was that she was loved and cherished. She was precious in her own right. She was precious because God created her and loved her.

You are precious too. I am precious. We are cherished, loved, valued because of who we are to God and who we are in Christ. We are his beloved daughters whose worth comes not from how attractive we are to men, but from God himself.

Bathsheba was indeed beautiful. But that is not the characteristic that God chose to focus on. Nathan doesn't liken her to a fattened calf, ripe for the slaughter. He doesn't even compare her to a grown sheep appropriate for a feast. Instead, she is just a lamb, meant to be loved.

The contrast between how God sees Bathsheba and how David sexualized her tells us that we don't have to buy the lie that our value is based on how desirable we are to men. We don't have to allow our body type, facial symmetry, skin condition, breast size, waist size, or any other physical feature to determine our self-worth, one way or the other. We don't have to succumb to sexualization. We may suffer the consequences of it, but we don't have to believe its lies.

Just as God saw the full humanity and beauty of Bathsheba, he sees the same in you. You are so much more than a sexual object. You are God's unique creation. Your beauty and worth are based not on your sexual appeal, but on God's love for you. God brought good out of Bathsheba's pain and loss, and he can do the same for you. But he will likely do it in a way that differs from the women of old.

In these stories of women in the Bible, it may seem that the only way a woman finds significance is by bearing children, particularly an important son. We might ask: Is that the only way women gain worth? No! It's important to remember that God often works within the confines of culture. In Old Testament days, bearing a son who rose to significance was viewed as the highest honor for a woman. God chose to honor these women, including Bathsheba, in a way they would recognize and appreciate.

Our culture is different. That's why for you and me, being redeemed and honored by God will most likely come in some other form. But one thing is clear—God views women as fully human, as complex and unique individuals. We are not sexual objects to be used and discarded. That was never God's intention for you. And in the wake of sexualization, God steps in. He rebukes, he saves, and he invites you to be so much more, to be all he created you to be.

Like Bathsheba, you, too, can overcome the sexualization in your past. You can live fiercely and fully and faithfully. You are more than your perceived desirability, or even lack of it.

You are a valued child of God, called for a purpose, bearing the very image of God.

> God created human beings in his own image. In the image of God he created them; male *and female* he created them. (Genesis 1:27 NLT, emphasis added)

You are an image-bearer of the Almighty God! The God of all the universe. The God who loves you.

> A really strong woman accepts the war she went through and is ennobled by her scars.
>
> Carly Simon

9

ESTHER

Dominated

Esther 1–9

For if you keep silent at this time, relief and deliverance will rise for the Jews from another place, but you and your father's house will perish. And who knows whether you have not come to the kingdom for such a time as this? (Esther 4:14)

--- • • • ---

To be dominated is to be controlled. Subject to another who plays the role of master. Sometimes it seems our lives, our destinies, our days, our nights, our past, our future are in the hands of a man who desires to dominate. We can feel helpless, hopeless, desperate, and afraid.

I sat across the table from her. I sipped my coffee. I listened. I fumed. "Don't tell me, he made you drop out."

She shrugged. "He said I didn't need college."

"And did you want to quit your job too?"

"Not really. He said I didn't need a job because he had one."

"And . . . ?"

For a moment, she closed her eyes. Her fingers wrapped around her paper coffee cup. "What am I going to do now? He controls everything. The money, the bank accounts. Even the car and credit cards are all in his name."

I leaned forward, my hand touching her knee. "It's going to be okay. You'll see. Don't be afraid. He wants you to be afraid."

I'd been listening for an hour, hearing a story that made my jaw tense with anger. We'd been friends for years, but I didn't know that her husband had dominated her so fully. She couldn't buy anything without his permission. She was told she was too stupid to get a job on her own, wasn't good enough to do anything but take care of their children in the way *he* wanted, couldn't go out unless he said it was okay, and the list went on and on.

Now, after ten years of marriage, he'd decided to get a girl-friend and leave his wife and family. For ten long years, she had lived in domination and fear, and now, with her confidence shattered, her faith in tatters, she had to decide if she would dare to take a risk and really live, really believe. She had a choice: Would she dare to become the woman God created her to be? Could she be bold? Could she be strong? Could she be smart and independent, fierce and confident? Could she be all the things her ex-husband had tried to defeat and deny in her?

She could. She is. In the year since we first sat down for coffee, I've watched my amazing friend take courageous step after courageous step. It's not been easy. There have been tears, frustration, hurt. But she presses forward. And she's learning she has power and abilities she never knew, given by God. She need not be afraid of the future. She need not be afraid of her ex. She can do more than just get by; she can flourish. And in doing so, she is protecting and paving the way for the children she loves to thrive as well.

In many ways, my friend reminds me of Esther. Dominated and living in fear. And yet, she somehow found the courage to face her fears and the man who dominated her. She rose up and became a woman of valor.

If Esther were to speak out today, I wonder how she might counsel us. What would she say about courage, about daring to do right even in the midst of domination? Perhaps she'd tell her story something like this . . .

ESTHER SPEAKS OUT

I didn't know. When Vashti defied the king and was deposed as queen, when the royal order went out to all the lands of the Persians and the Medes that every man was master in his own household, I certainly didn't know. When they took me from my home to the king's harem, when they made me the king's concubine and I spent a year in beautification—oil of myrrh, spices, ointments, and cosmetics—when Hegai, the king's eunuch, advanced me to the best place in the harem, I still didn't know. Even when I went in to the king and found favor with him, when I was chosen to be queen and the crown set on my head, still I believed I had no power. I had no choice but to obey or die.

I hid my heritage, I lowered my gaze, I took nothing with me from the first harem to the second, only what Hegai advised. Nothing of my own. I made no decisions. I offered no resistance.

But I watched, and I waited. And I tried to be wise.

My cousin, Mordecai, checked on me every day. He advised me, just as he had during all my growing up years since my parents had died and he took me in as his own. I listened to him because he always counseled what he thought best for me, to help me, protect me, so I would flourish, even in the precarious position of queen.

So when I heard he had torn his clothes and put on sackcloth and ashes, I was alarmed. When I discovered he was at the entrance of the king's gate, dressed in sackcloth when no one was allowed to enter that gate wearing sackcloth, I sent garments to clothe him. But the servants returned to me, clothes in hand, saying he had refused them.

I sent Hathach, the eunuch attending me, to inquire of Mordecai. The man who had sought to keep me safe should not now be almost breaking the law sitting in sackcloth right at my very gate!

Hathach came back with horrific news. It had been decreed that my people, the Jews, were to be slaughtered. My husband the king had unwittingly given them into the hand of Haman, his official, and the royal decree had already been sent out. The whole land had been instructed to destroy, to kill, and to annihilate all Jews, young and old, women and children, in one day, the thirteenth day of the twelfth month.

I could barely breathe at the horror of it.

But there was more. Mordecai had sent an instruction, a command, for me. I was to go to the king to beg his favor and plead with him on behalf of my people.

I had always followed Mordecai's guidance. I had always obeyed the king. But now, what power did I have to change the mind of the king? I trembled. I knew the law. I knew the consequences for approaching the king without being called. I knew my place. I knew how to be safe.

But I didn't know the truth. Not yet.

I spoke to Hathach and commanded him to go to Mordecai, to say, "All the king's servants and the people of the king's provinces know that if any man or woman goes to the king inside the inner court without being called, there is but one law—to be put to death, except the one to whom the king holds out the golden scepter so that he may live. But as for me, I have not been called to come in to the king these thirty days."

Didn't he know I was powerless? The position of queen held no authority, no special access, no real influence at all. Where would I get the authority I needed to approach a king?

I didn't know.

Mordecai's reply came back to me: "Do not think to yourself that in the king's palace you will escape any more than all the other Jews. For if you keep silent at this time, relief and deliverance will rise for the Jews from another place, but you and your father's house will perish. And who knows whether you have not come to the kingdom for such a time as this?"

For such a time as this?

What did I know? How could I, a powerless woman, make a difference in a world where women held no power, and where Jews now held even less?

A woman. A Jew. A queen.

Helpless. Powerless. Choice-less.

Or was I?

I motioned for the messenger to wait.

I felt helpless. But I knew One who helped his people.

I felt powerless. But I knew One who had more power even than a king.

Choice-less? Maybe. But maybe not. Choices, after all, are granted not by a king, not even by men, but by God himself.

I lifted my chin and steeled myself against the wave of fear that washed over me. Then, I spoke my message back to Mordecai: "Go, gather all the Jews to be found in Susa, and hold a fast on my behalf, and do not eat or drink for three days, night or day. I and my young women will also fast as you do. Then I will go to the king, though it is against the law, and if I perish, I perish."

My attendants and I fasted for three days. I fought a battle between faithfulness and fear. And after three days, I won.

Servants helped me put on my royal robes. My hands shook as they fastened them around my shoulders. I left my chambers without a glance behind me, and I walked toward the king's quarters. I stopped in the inner court of the king's palace, in front of his quarters, while the king was sitting within on his royal throne opposite the entrance to the palace.

I stood. I waited. I prayed.

The king saw me.

I held my breath. I counted.

One, two, three, four. The longest moments of my life.

And then, he held out to me the golden scepter that was in his hand.

I felt the power surge through me, not my own power, but the power of the God of the Jews, the power of a God who listens to the cries of his people. A God who sees, hears, knows, and remembers that we are but dust.

I was powerless. He was not.

I approached and touched the tip of the king's scepter.

"What is it, Queen Esther?" the king asked. "What is your request? It shall be given you, even to the half of my kingdom."

I almost asked then and there that he save my people. I almost requested that the half a kingdom be for the Jews. But I kept to the plan that had formed in my mind as I had waited and hoped and feared. As I had fasted and prayed. And I believed that not Mordecai, not the king, not the eunuchs or advisors, but God himself had given me that plan.

"If it please the king," I said, "let the king and Haman come today to a feast that I have prepared for the king."

Then, I bowed and left. I had a feast to prepare, not just of food but of hope and daring.

Later, both men came to the feast. And the king asked again about my wish. I didn't know why God would have me delay, but it didn't seem the time was yet right to make my request. So I asked both men to come again to a feast that I would prepare the next day.

The morrow came and I heard that Haman had made gallows, fifty cubits high, so that he might hang Mordecai. But while Haman was making plans for my family's destruction, it must be that God was making other plans. For the king, on that very night, had not been able to sleep and so he called for the chronicles of the kingdom to be read, and from that he was reminded of how Mordecai had saved the king from conspiracy.

While Haman hoped for a hanging, the king declared that he would honor Mordecai. And in a great reversal only God could orchestrate, Haman was commanded to dress Mordecai in the king's robes and led him through the square of the city on the king's horse, proclaiming before him, "Thus shall it be done to the man whom the king delights to honor."

Then I understood why I had to wait. Surely God had a better plan in store.

Later on that same day, as the king and Haman were drinking wine after the feast, the king said to me again, "What is your wish, Queen Esther? It shall be granted you. And what is your request? Even to the half of my kingdom, it shall be fulfilled."

And this time, I answered. "If I have found favor in your sight, O king, and if it please the king, let my life be granted me for my wish, and my people for my request. For we have been sold, I and my people, to be destroyed, to be killed, and to be annihilated. If we had been sold merely as slaves, men and women, I would have been silent, for our affliction is not to be compared with the loss to the king."

Then, I held my breath and waited.

The king rose in his seat. "Who is he, and where is he, who has dared to do this?"

My moment had come. I straightened my shoulders and pointed to the enemy of my people. "A foe and enemy! This wicked Haman!"

The king stormed from the table and went into the palace garden. I thought Haman would follow him. Instead, the vile man fell on the couch where I was reclining. He begged for his life, pawed at me in his distress. He cared only for saving himself. He did not repent of his evil.

Then, the king returned. "Will he even assault the queen in my presence, in my own house?"

As the words left the mouth of the king, men in attendance covered Haman's face. Then Harbona, one of the eunuchs who served the king, said, "Moreover, the gallows that Haman has prepared for Mordecai, whose word saved the king, is standing at Haman's house, fifty cubits high."

And the king said, "Hang him on that."

So they hanged Haman on the gallows that he had prepared for Mordecai. Then the wrath of the king abated.

But my people were still in danger.

The king gave me Haman's property. He brought Mordecai before him and set him over the house of Haman.

And yet, the edict to kill my people still remained.

So I went once more before the king. I dared again to approach uninvited.

I fell at his feet and wept and pleaded with him to avert the evil plan of Haman the Agagite and the plot that he had devised against the Jews.

When the king again held out to me the golden scepter, I rose and said, "If it please the king, and if I have found favor in his sight, and if the thing seems right before the king, and I am pleasing in his eyes, let an order be written to revoke the letters devised by Haman the Agagite, the son of Hammedatha, which he wrote to destroy the Jews who are in all the provinces of the king. For how can I bear to see the calamity that is coming to my people? Or how can I bear to see the destruction of my kindred?"

The king said to me, "You may write as you please with regard to the Jews, in the name of the king, and seal it with the king's ring, for an edict written in the name of the king and sealed with the king's ring cannot be revoked."

I closed my eyes as relief washed over me. I knew just what the new decree should say to save my people.

The scribes were summoned, and an edict went out, sealed by the king's signet ring, saying that the king allowed the Jews who were in every city to gather and defend their lives, to destroy, to kill, and to annihilate any armed force of any people or province that might attack them, children and women included, and to plunder their goods, on the same day that the previous edict had named for their destruction.

And there was great rejoicing in all the city when they learned of the new statute. I could hear their shouts of joy even from the palace.

The twelfth month, the month of Adar, came, and with it came the thirteenth day of the month, the day meant for our destruction. The day God had changed from a death sentence into a celebration of redemption. So on that day meant for our annihilation, there was gladness and joy, a feast and a holiday. And my people, who had no power, gained mastery over their enemies and all who hated them.

This was the first celebration of the feast of Purim, a holiday my people have celebrated ever since. And I, the daughter of Abihail, a woman and a Jew, found that I had power after all. The power to serve, the power to dare, the power to risk my life for the lives of my people.

I didn't know. My life had seemed ruled by men. I believed I had no choices, no freedom, no agency of my own. I believed I was powerless.

But now I know. I know the truth.

God always gives us the power to do right. My choice was whether or not to use it.

Dominated

We know the outcome of the story, and so we typically read the book of Esther as the account of a brave heroine. What we sometimes overlook, however, is that Esther was a woman who was dominated by men. She was taken from her home, placed in a dangerous situation, and every choice, action, moment of her life was controlled by men, especially the king, whose authority could not be crossed upon fear of death. Sometimes we too feel powerless in the face of overpowering men. But Esther's experience tells another story. And she reaches out her hand to every woman who has been dominated, inviting us to step out of fear and into courage and faithfulness to God. She tells us we have a choice—and with that choice comes power.

No Choices?

We have choices. You have choices. Do you have to submit to abuse? Do you have to believe lies? Do you have to cower and tolerate and suffer? Do you have to be silent? Do you have to "protect" your kids by behaving in a way that suggests it's okay to tolerate demeaning comments, abusive behavior, neglect, and prejudice?

Or is there a better way, even if it might be risky?

Esther initially believed she had no choices, no power. Intervention to save her people could easily have cost her life and still not prevented the slaughter. The values and practices of her culture told her to stay silent, play it safe. Keep herself out of harm's way.

Faith, however, told her something different. Faith gave a different call.

Mordecai said to her, "For if you keep silent at this time, relief and deliverance will rise for the Jews from another place, but you and your father's house will perish. And who knows whether you have not come to the kingdom for such a time as this?" (Esther 4:14).

Esther had a choice. Silence and perceived safety, or action and risk.

It wasn't a simple choice or an easy one, but she did have the power to choose, even in the face of danger and fear.

Mordecai firmly believed that deliverance *would* come. God is always on the side of righteousness. He is always at work on behalf of his people. The question was, would Esther, will we, partner with God in that redemptive work. Will we dare? Will we step out? Will we speak up for what's right?

Will you, like Esther, be brave enough to be a part of God's redemptive work?

Will you use the power you have to make a choice that only you can make?

Will you choose faithfulness over fear?

Faithfulness and Fear

It's not easy choice. It's never easy to do the right thing in the right way, especially when we've been conditioned to play it safe, to avoid rocking the boat, to believe we are powerless.

Abusers know how to make you feel worthless and weak, to make you believe there's nothing you can do to improve your situation. They know how to pressure you into feeling that you are lesser, not good enough, and certainly not strong enough, wise enough, or holy enough to oppose them. That's the goal—to make you live the lie.

But how could you, a daughter of the King, beloved and treasured by the Creator of the universe, be powerless? Worthless? Less? How could you possibly be not enough?

Impossible!

Esther's culture conditioned her to submit to powerful men. But the One who loved her and her people had all the power. She appealed to him through fasting. She asked for others to join her in this appeal. Together with her people, she sought the wisdom and guidance of the true King.

Haman believed he had gained all the power he needed. But it was God who was in control. Through King Ahasuerus, God himself stretched out the golden scepter to Esther. Esther was given the power she needed to survive, thrive, and save those she loved.

God stretches out the scepter to you, too. The scepter of welcome, of acceptance, of empowerment. God doesn't leave you powerless. Though everything around her told her she had no power, Esther did have power to choose. God gave her that power. She had everything she needed to pursue justice, to seek mercy for her people, to prevent a great evil.

Faithfulness or fear? The choice is ours. Sometimes, we simply have to take a holy risk.

Holy Risks

Esther had a choice. She could have chosen safety by saying nothing. Maybe the king wouldn't have found out she was a Jew. But silence isn't always as safe as it sounds. God will not forever tolerate injustice, abuse, or evil. The Hamans of the world will be confronted, called to account, condemned. God always works, in his timing, to eliminate evil. As Mordecai asserts, God will provide relief and deliverance one way or another.

The safest choice is the one that puts you in the center of God's will. When you're afraid of what God has called you to do and tempted to choose safety instead, it's good to remember that safety also poses a risk. An *unholy* risk.

Holy risk, however, is something else entirely. It is taking the risk to follow God even when you're afraid. It is seeking him, watching for him, and walking in the path he sets for you, no matter how much you feel trapped or powerless. It is stepping forward to do right, to protect yourself and others, even when you wonder whether or not you have what it takes.

Holy risk is about daring to believe that God stands with you, has gone before you to make a way, just as he did for Esther. It is also about getting help from others. All the Jews in the capital of Susa fasted with Esther for three days. The eunuchs helped Esther. The messengers helped her. Her women fasted with her. When she went before the king, she was physically alone, but she was not alone in any other way. A whole people stood behind her, supporting her.

And while the book of Esther never specifically mentions God, prayer, or faith, we see evidence of God's intervention and Esther's faith nonetheless. Mordecai believed that deliverance would come for the Jews and that Esther's position in the palace was no accident. Esther called for a time of fasting, which, for the Jews, would have the sole purpose of calling on God and submitting to Him. So even without mention of God, God was clearly present. And faith was revealed—not only Esther's faith but the faith of Mordecai and the Jewish people.

So when Esther approached the king, she did so not in her own power but in the power of God, prepared for her by the faith of her own fasting, her people's fasting, and the fasting of the women around her. And because of that, her holy risk reflected the nature of God, a nature steeped in love. The apostle Paul describes such love when he writes, "Love is patient and kind; love does not envy or boast; it is not arrogant or rude. It does not insist on its own way; it is not irritable or resentful; it does not rejoice at wrongdoing, but rejoices with the truth. Love bears all things, believes all things, hopes all things, endures all things" (1 Corinthians 13:4–7). It's not hard to recognize these characteristics in Esther's demeanor and choices.

Esther's appeal to the king was patient (she took several days to prepare and then state her plea). It was kind and deferential instead of arrogant. It was respectful and not rude. She did not insist that the king do as she asked through an attempt to assert her own dominance; rather, she acknowledged the position of the king and simply told him the truth about the evil planned for her people. We do not see her envying his position or even Haman's, or boasting of her own position. She claimed no rights as queen. She agonized at the injustice her people would suffer and rejoiced (with all the Jews) when the truth was revealed.

She dared to approach the king. She acted in God's power and not her own. She asked for help. She hoped. She endured.

She took a holy risk.

Perhaps you, like Esther, were made for such a time as this. A time to dare for the sake of righteousness, for the sake of those you love. For yourself.

Perhaps it's time to take a holy risk.

Who Is God When We're Dominated?

God created human beings and dared to empower them to make choices. Good or bad. He knew the risk; he planned for the outcome. He sent his beloved Son, who dared to die in order to save us all.

The religious leaders of Jesus's day tried to dominate him. Herod did the same. Pilate washed his hands of him. Nevertheless, he was arrested, beaten, and crucified. And then he rose again. He rose in the power of God, the power that turned death into life. Eternal life. New, vigorous, never-to-die-again life!

And he makes that eternal life available to you. And that life empowers us. So that you can dare to rise, too, in a different sense. Dare to speak. Dare to believe that life can be, should be, whatever it is God calls you to. You have choices. And you have power, God's power. The same power that raised Jesus from the dead. The apostle Paul—who endured persecution and physical suffering—dared to proclaim, "I can do all things through him who strengthens me" (Philippians 4:13). It's a verse that's so familiar to most of us that it's lost some of its impact. It sounds rather unimpressive, as if God simply makes our own miniscule power a little bit stronger. However, the original Greek in which this verse was written gives us a different view.

The root of the Greek word translated "strengthens" is *endynamoo*, a compound of the words *en* and *dynamoo*. *Dynamoo* is the verb form of the noun *dynamis*, which means power, might, strength. It is the source from which we get the English word *dynamite*. *En* is a preposition typically meaning "in" or "into." So *endynamoo* means to put power into. A more literal translation of Paul's statement then would be, *I can do all things through him who empowers me, who puts his power into me.* God quite literally places his power into you and me. And it is no small power. It is dynamite power!

So, still think you can't do it? That you're not brave enough, strong enough, smart enough, powerful enough? You're probably right. Esther wasn't "enough" either. But just like her, you don't have to do it alone. It's not your power that matters. It's God's power in you that makes the difference. And he is more than enough.

Take courage! You may have been pushed down, demeaned, told you don't know anything, can't do anything. You may have been conditioned to be dependent. But God is calling you to dare—to step out of your safety zone and into his power. To walk in the confidence of his *dynamoo* power in you.

The choice is yours: faithfulness or fear. Will you dare to take a holy risk with the empowering God who raised Jesus from the dead? Will you dare to live confident and unafraid?

> You gain strength, courage, and confidence by every experience in which you really stop to look fear in the face. You are able to say to yourself, "I lived through this horror. I can take the next thing that comes along."
>
> Eleanor Roosevelt

10

MARY AND MARTHA

Oppressed

Luke 10

Martha, Martha, you are anxious and troubled
about many things, but one thing is necessary.
Mary has chosen the good portion, which will
not be taken away from her. (Luke 10:41–42)

Oppressed. It means to be pushed down, restrained, sup-
pressed, subjugated. Sometimes it's hard to break free
of oppressive expectations and demands. And sometimes that
oppression comes from places, from people we don't expect.
From those who are supposed to be our allies and friends.
From other women.

—————— • • • ——————

My hand shook as I stood at the kitchen sink with the letter clutched in my fist. It seemed innocuous enough—just a

note from the pastor's wife, signed by her and her husband, urging women to volunteer in children's ministry at church. Just a little letter, sweetly worded, but also heaped with "you shoulds" and "you oughts" and other pressure tactics to get women of the church, especially young moms, to do their duty as Christian women, just as she had done when her kids were young.

There I stood, round with child number five, with three-year-old twins and two other little ones a bit older. I was harried. I was tired. I was beyond tired. Deeply weary in body and soul.

But none of that seemed to matter to the pastor and his wife. Six-and-a-half days a week, I took care of my own little kids. Now I was expected to give up the half day I had at church to take care of other people's children as well. And we weren't being asked, not really. Instead, it felt like we were being guilted. Manipulated. The letter basically said that if we were good Christian women, if we really were faithful and holy, then surely we would volunteer on Sundays. At least once a month. After all, that's simply what was expected of women!

My longing for Christ, my desire to have one undistracted morning to seek him? Did that matter? Wanting to sit at Jesus's feet and learn more about him together with my community once a week? Did my pastor's wife appreciate that? Yearning to worship without little ones clinging to my legs for a change? Did anyone care about that? All that seemed to matter was that as a good Christian woman I should volunteer for children's ministry. *Period.*

All these years later, I'm willing to give the pastor's wife a small benefit of the doubt, to assume that she meant well and had the best interests of the church at heart. But the manipulative way she went about it felt like a spiritualized form of oppression—an unjust and burdensome use of power. How could this come from another woman who had been where I was? How could it come from a woman who knew what it was like to try to be all things to all people with littles hanging on your legs? How could someone who was supposed to be my ally—who was supposed to "get it" and have my back—treat me this way?

I wish I could say that I didn't succumb to the manipulation. I'd like to say that, but it wouldn't be true. Mentally, I wrote dozens of blistering letters saying everything I wanted to say, but I never put them to paper, much less sent them. And, sad to say, I did sign up to volunteer in the children's ministry once a month.

On those Sundays, I didn't have just two screaming three-year-olds, I had twenty. And nothing about my service filled me with the peace of Christ. Probably because Jesus hadn't invited me into that ministry in the first place. Instead, another woman had pressured and guilted me with shoulds and oughts until I succumbed to her expectations rather than honoring the longings of my soul for time with Christ.

Since then, I've thought long about the oppression of, and the expectations placed on, women in the church by other women. I've thought about those Sundays when I was in the three-year-old class and my heart cried out for something different, for a real encounter with Jesus in my kid-laden life, and the women in charge should have known better, should have cared better.

A simple letter coercing me into an unwanted role may not seem like it fits the definition of oppression. And let's be honest, in comparison to the horrific abuse suffered by many, it hardly qualifies. Yet there is something particularly discouraging and burdensome when other women—Christian women—guilt or shame us, manipulate us, or try to force us into complying with roles or expectations.

Today, as I think back on my own experiences of woman-to-woman oppression, it is the story of Mary and her sister Martha that comes to mind. Two women, both of whom were loved by Jesus. But who, in at least one instance, had very different views of what it really meant to love him in return. If we listen to Mary tell her story, it might sound something like this . . .

MARY SPEAKS OUT

There was an ache in me so deep and so strong it was almost painful. I yearned to spend time with him, Jesus, the rabbi from Nazareth, our friend. I thirsted, hungered, to hear his words, be in his presence. To simply sit at his feet and listen to his teaching. His words were like the finest bread to me, his presence the sweetest wine.

My sister, always the responsible one, had different longings. Martha knew her duty. She knew her role. She knew what it meant to be a respectable and responsible woman in our culture, in our time. And in a way, she was right.

So when Jesus entered our village, Martha went directly out to meet him and welcomed him into her house. Our house. Once the rabbi and his disciples were settled, she hustled to prepare food, wine, everything expected of a good hostess.

Still, I could tell she was harried and distressed. I could tell she wanted everything to be perfect. And everything was. Everything, that is, except me.

Instead of taking my expected place serving at her side, I sat at the Lord's feet and listened to his teaching. I dared to defy every expectation of what a woman, a hostess, should be. Instead of serving, I drank deeply of his words. And my soul was filled.

Martha's wasn't. My choice was so unthinkable and offensive, it violated her sense of right and wrong. My sister hurried to the teacher, her face flush with anger. "Lord, do you not care that my sister has left me to serve alone? Tell her then to help me."

For a moment, I held my breath. What would he say? Were the expectations of my role as a woman more important than sitting at the feet of my Lord? My sister thought so. But something deep within me rebelled at the thought that because I was a woman, I could serve and help but never be nearer to him than offering a plate of food or pouring a cup of wine.

My sister, who loved the rabbi as much as I did, nevertheless wanted me to fill the role of traditional Jewish women, a role she had chosen and embraced for herself.

Jesus looked long at Martha, his expression neither angry or surprised. Then he answered, his voice so gentle that it rang through my soul like a call from the heavens. "Martha, Martha, you are anxious and troubled about many things, but one thing is necessary. Mary has chosen the good portion, which will not be taken away from her."

It will not be taken away. I almost laughed. I had chosen well!

Somehow, in those few words, my Lord and teacher had set me free. I could be the woman I wanted to be. I could be a follower of this rabbi called Jesus. I could be more than a hostess, more than a server of food and wine, more than what my culture said was possible for a woman. I could be a disciple of Jesus from Nazareth.

I glanced at my sister. Her brows furrowed. She was thinking. She was always thinking. And I wondered how she would respond to the Teacher's words. Would she who sought to coerce me into something I did not want now join me at the feet of Jesus and soaking in his words of life?

Oppressed

When we think of the oppression of women, we typically confine our thoughts to the actions of men against women. Historically, it is predominately men who are the oppressors. However, we also need to consider those times when other women not only fall short of being our allies but contribute to our burdens. We need to take an honest look at the oppression caused by the misperceptions not only of men but of the women who are closest to us, even those we've been taught to look up to. Because sometimes the shame we feel comes from the words and actions of other women. Because sometimes women act more like oppressors than sisters. And that hurts.

Why Do Women Do That?

We should be supporting each other, helping each other, encouraging each other to be all we can be in Christ. Right? So why isn't that always the case? Why is it that other women sometimes pressure us to fit into a role or a stereotype based on cultural expectations or whatever has been traditionally considered acceptable?

The answer is simple: Sin. One of the reasons vocational psychologist Meredith Fuller gives as to why women oppress other women is because a woman is projecting her own "fear, envy, jealousy, suspicion, resentment, rage," and so on onto the other woman.[1] A woman may assert power over another woman in order to alleviate her own fears of powerlessness. She may be acting out of her own resentment of feeling pressured to fit cultural molds for women. If she gives in to the pressure to adopt traditional cultural roles, she may in turn pressure other women to do the same.

Women married to men in ministry are frequently pressured to fit into and live up to everyone else's expectations of who they should be. Some who fail to meet these expectations are told that their shortcomings or choices reflect poorly on their husband's ministry performance and could cost him his job. Women, hear me. Each of us, whether in ministry or not, is carefully and uniquely shaped by God to fit his vision, not a cultural mold or one-size-fits-all role, and certainly not one based on unrealistic "ideals" from decades past.

Martha, too, may have lashed out at Mary, pressuring her to serve instead of sit at Jesus's feet, because of internal resentments resulting from the pressure to live up to cultural norms for women. Perhaps she felt envy, jealousy, resentment, even rage. Perhaps she would have liked to defy the cultural expectations tied to her position and sit at Jesus's feet herself. But she didn't. She felt she had to serve. She had to be the good hostess.

She, Mary, and their brother Lazarus were counted among Jesus's closest friends. Martha loved Jesus dearly and frequently opened her home to him. I don't think it's unreasonable to think that she too would have loved to learn from him as her sister Mary did.

But she chose not to. The cultural demands of hospitality and the expectations everyone had of her were too great. Women were to serve men. Women did not, under any circumstance, sit and learn from rabbis. It was unheard of! In fact, a rabbi quoted in the Mishnah, a compilation of Jewish rabbinic teachings dating from 200 BC to AD 200, states, "If a man gives his daughter knowledge of the law it is as though he taught her lechery."[2] Martha knew her proper place. But I suspect, deep inside, she resented it.

And so, when Mary flouted the same cultural expectations that were burdening Martha, Martha was indignant. How dare Mary not toe the line and serve the men! How dare she sit and learn at the rabbi's feet as if she were a man! Martha's own frustrated, unfulfilled longing may have caused her to lash out against her sister and demand that she satisfy the expected role of serving the men.

Unlike many of us, however, Mary did not succumb to her sister's pressure to meet other people's expectations. She didn't jump up and start serving. She didn't apologize. She didn't allow a fear of disapproval from others to influence her actions. She simply let Jesus answer for her. She waited to see what *he* would say, how *he* would direct her, what *he* thought best for her.

She didn't defend herself. She let Jesus do that. And in so doing, she discovered Jesus did not adhere to those cultural roles and expectations of women that Martha was working so hard to live up to. Instead, he affirmed that a woman's place, just like a man's, was at the feet of her Savior and God.

Martha was welcome there too. But first she would have to let go of burdensome expectations placed on her by others because of gender. She would have to choose between what she thought everyone else wanted from her and what she really wanted for herself—a relationship with Jesus.

In his response to her appeal, Jesus essentially invites Martha to make that choice.

What We Really Want

Mary knew what she really wanted. She wanted to learn from Jesus, to be close to him, to hear his words and sit at his feet. And that's just what she did, despite the harsh words and expectations of her sister, the woman closest to her, and a fellow follower of Jesus.

I suspect that Martha wanted the same thing, but she didn't know it. The desire to do what others expected of her, to make sure she was doing everything right, to make sure everything was "just so" for her guests, obscured the deeper desires of her heart. And the result wasn't pretty. She was so rushed and frustrated she even confronted Jesus, the rabbi she loved, and made accusations against him. She told him what he ought to do! "Lord, do you not care that my sister has left me to serve alone? Tell her then to help me" (Luke 10:40).

Jesus was gentle in his rebuke. "Martha, Martha, you are anxious and troubled about many things," he said, "but one thing is necessary. Mary has chosen the good portion, which will not be taken away from her" (Luke 10:41–42). According to author Michael Card, "'It will not be taken away from her,' translates into, 'So, no, I will not tell her to leave her place.'"[3] Mary found her place. *Her* place. And it wasn't the place where women were typically encouraged to be, or even allowed to be. But Jesus would not permit cultural expectations, gender roles, or pressure from others—even his other followers—to displace her.

Just like Mary, who chose well, and like Martha, who was anxious and troubled about many things, we too are presented with a choice. Will we choose to fit into what we think we "have to do" and "have to be," or will we choose to sit at Jesus's feet and become not merely "a good Christian woman," but a fully devoted disciple?

According to John Cassian, a monk born in AD 360, "To cling always to God and to the things of God—this must be our major effort, this must be the road that the heart follows unswervingly. Any diversion, however impressive, must be regarded as secondary, low-grade and certainly dangerous."[4] In other words, we must focus on the things of God, on sitting at his feet, learning from him. Allowing ourselves to be pressured into living up to other people's expectations of what a woman, especially a Christian woman, is supposed to be and do is a distraction. It will take us further away from, rather than closer to, the woman God created each of us to be.

It is not a kindness to others to try to meet their unrealistic or misguided expectations of who we should be. No, that is hazardous to the health of our souls. And it is not the thing that Jesus says is necessary for us. It is not "the good portion" that Mary chose and that Jesus offers to each of us.

Mary or Martha?

Perhaps you have been a victim of a Martha in your life. Perhaps you've been pressured to fit into a traditional or limited view of what a female follower of Christ is supposed to be—to smile, serve, be everything for everybody all the time. To follow instead of lead. To use your gifts only for children's and women's ministries. To silently submit to those roles held only by men.

And never sit at Jesus's feet. That's not your place.

Except it is. Jesus says so.

When another woman pressures, "Why aren't you doing what you're supposed to?" remember, there was no rebuke for Mary from Jesus. She found her place at Jesus's feet, she chose to remain there, and Jesus would not allow her place to be taken from her.

And Martha? Jesus offered her an invitation as well—an invitation to let go of other people's expectations. She too could choose to sit at Jesus's feet and feed her soul. We see a hint in John 11 that she considered Jesus's invitation and, somewhere along the way, accepted it.

When her brother Lazarus died, Martha broke with traditional mourning customs to go out to meet Jesus:

When Martha heard that Jesus was coming, she went and met him, but Mary remained seated in the house. Martha said to Jesus, "Lord, if you had been here, my brother would not have died. But even now I know that whatever you ask from God, God will give you." Jesus said to her, "Your brother will rise again." Martha said to him, "I know that he will rise again in the resurrection on the last day." Jesus said to her, "I am the resurrection and the life. Whoever believes in me, though he die, yet shall he live, and everyone who lives and believes in me shall never die. Do you believe this?" She said to him, "Yes, Lord; I believe that you are the Christ, the Son of God, who is coming into the world." (John 11:20–27)

Regardless of the circumstances, and regardless of what other people expect, choosing to be near to Jesus and to listen to him is always the best choice. And on this occasion, it was Martha who chose the better portion.

Jesus defends our right to seek him, to be who he made us to be. We don't have to pretend to be the model Christian woman. We only have to truly love the One who longs to give us the better portion. When we choose to be with him, we can stand in faith, even in our darkest moments, and say with Martha, "Yes, Lord; I believe that you are the Christ, the Son of God, who is coming into the world." When the taunts and disparagement of others threaten our peace, we can remember that Jesus came to redeem us and make us his own. When we feel hurt and humiliated, we can remember that Jesus has saved and rescued us. When we feel less than, that we've somehow failed, that we don't measure up, we can still say, "Yes, Lord. I believe that you have come into *my* world to save and set me free."

Who Is God When We're Oppressed?

Jesus never calls us to meet the expectations of others. In fact, he often challenged the legalisms held by the religious leaders of his day. They had their traditions, their expectations, their interpretations of what they believed was God's law and God's way. But Jesus never condoned their narrow interpretations and beliefs. In fact, he routinely challenged them, such as on this occasion when his disciples failed to meet the requirements of ceremonial law:

> Now when the Pharisees gathered to him, with some of the scribes who had come from Jerusalem, they saw that some of his disciples ate with hands that were defiled, that is, unwashed. (For the Pharisees and all the Jews do not eat unless they wash their hands properly, holding to the tradition of the elders. . . . And there are many other traditions that they observe. . . .) And the Pharisees and the scribes asked him, "Why do your disciples not walk according to the tradition of the elders, but eat with defiled hands?" And he said to them, "Well did Isaiah prophesy of you hypocrites, as it is written,
>
> "'This people honors me with their lips,
>   but their heart is far from me;
> in vain do they worship me,
>   teaching as doctrines the commandments of
>   men.'
>
> "You leave the commandment of God and hold to the tradition of men."
>   And he said to them, "You have a fine way of rejecting the commandment of God in order to establish your tradition!" (Mark 7:1–9)

Tradition. Often what others insist is biblical, or God's way, is really only human tradition, cultural tradition, or "the way things have always been." When Jesus came, he shattered many of these traditions—not only ceremonial traditions, such as the washing of hands, but also social traditions about the roles and expectations placed on women.

A woman sitting and learning at a rabbi's feet? *Scandalous!*

Women disciples, such as Mary Magdalene, Mary and Martha, and others? *Radical!*

Women as the first witnesses to the resurrection? *Unheard of!*

When he walked the earth, Jesus was not a traditional rabbi. He was not even a what-was-expected Messiah. Instead, he chose to be exactly who God the Father wanted him to be.

You can be the woman God wants you to be. You can be Mary, choosing to sit at the feet of Jesus. You can be Martha, who accepted Jesus's invitation to set aside the expectations of others.

Jesus himself longs to say of you, "She has chosen the good portion, which will not be taken away from her."

> How sweet, the presence of Jesus to the longing, harassed soul! It is instant peace, and balm to every wound.
>
> Elizabeth Ann Seton

11

A SAMARITAN WOMAN
Shamed

John 4

Come, see a man who told me all that I ever did.
Can this be the Christ? (John 4:29)

Shamed. It is to be self-conscious, battered by disgrace and sometimes self-loathing. Shame comes when the humiliation of what another has done to us, or what we have done in response, rises up like a living thing within us. It whispers or screams that we are unworthy, dirty, disgraced, despicable. We must hide to cover our unworthiness. The pain of shame can dig deeper than any physical wound. It can warp not only our thoughts, but our very lives.

• • •

She stood at the front of the room telling a story of how neighbor boys had repeatedly jumped her on her way home from school, dragged her into a shed, and raped her. The room was mournfully silent as she told just the barest details of her story. Then she spoke of how these childhood experiences had stained her for life. Other predators continued to seek her out, as if they could sense she was easy prey.

For years, she felt haunted by her past, convinced she would never be whole. But then she encountered Jesus in a way she hadn't before. She'd known him, accepted him, but it took time for him to reach those deeply wounded places of shame and hurt. It took time for him to heal the scars caused by horrific and repeated abuse. But in time, it happened. Jesus replaced her scars with his scars. He replaced the markers of damage with the mark of his healing, his grace, his freedom to be who she really was. Now, she was no longer shamed. She was unblemished, loved, cherished, and whole. She was a powerful spokeswoman for God's love to others who had been abused.

When she finished speaking, women poured toward the platform to embrace her and to share their own stories. And that day, I saw chains of shame shattered all over that room. I saw women set free to live, to love, and to be—to *fully* be.

In this woman who courageously shared her story, I saw someone who reminded me of the Samaritan woman at the well—a woman whose shame was transformed into a beacon of healing light pointing others to Christ. And I wonder, if the Samaritan woman could speak out today, what might she say about her own encounter with Jesus? Perhaps her story would go something like this . . .

A SAMARITAN WOMAN SPEAKS OUT

I carry an empty water jar to the well at noonday. In the heat of the day, when I will meet no one, see no one, encounter no one.

But oh, it's hot in the middle of the day, and the dust swirls at my feet. Sweat gathers on my brow.

I am lonely. The words trickle through my mind. I dismiss them. Ignore them. I am fine. Everything is fine. It does not matter that I go for water in the heat of the day when no else is at the well. It doesn't matter. I don't care.

Except I do.

In the distance, I hear male voices, Galilean, I think. I look up to see men sauntering toward me. I turn my face away and hurry past. They don't take notice of me.

No one ever does. I am invisible. I am nobody. I tell myself I like it that way.

I lie.

The other women come to the well early, in the cool of the morning. They gossip and laugh and talk about their lives and their hopes and their plans for the day.

I come when the sun is at its zenith. And I come alone. Draw water alone. Leave alone.

As I approach the well, I look up and then stop short.

A man, a Jew, sits at the edge. *Oh no.* It's best if I avoid men even more than I avoid the other women coming to the well. But I need water. I need it desperately.

I adjust the empty jar under my arm and scuttle to the far side of the well. I remind myself that I am invisible. He will not notice me.

Except he does. Perhaps I am not as invisible as I pretend to be.

"Give me a drink."

I swallow and my world stills. He spoke to me. Why did he speak to me? I glance around and then at him. I gather my courage around me like a coat of thistles. Prickly. Hard. But I am curious. I am a Samaritan. I am a woman—and not a good woman at that. My brows furrow. What kind of strange man is this before me? A question spills from my lips before I can stop it. "How is it that you, a Jew, ask for a drink from me, a woman of Samaria?"

He looks at me, straight in the eyes. As if I am not just a woman, not a despised Samaritan, as if I don't mask a hidden humiliation. "If you knew the gift of God, and who it is that is saying to you, 'Give me a drink,' you would have asked him, and he would have given you living water."

Why does he speak of running water? Is it a riddle? Is it some kind of insult? I lift my chin, steady my voice. I may not be a solver of riddles, but I am used to insults. I did not come to the well to play games with words. "Sir, you have nothing to draw water with, and the well is deep. Where do you get that living water? Are you greater than our father Jacob? He gave us the well and drank from it himself, as did his sons and his livestock."

He smiles, ever so slightly. "Anyone who drinks this water will soon become thirsty again. But those who drink the water I give will never be thirsty again. It becomes a fresh, bubbling spring within them, giving them eternal life."

He is bluffing. Men don't give women water. Men don't serve women. And yet, he is speaking to me, a Samaritan woman. And he has asked only for sip of water to drink. I will call his bluff.

"Sir, give me this water, so that I will not be thirsty or have to come here to draw water." For a moment, I envision what it would be like to be freed from this daily march of shame. No more whispers. No more sneaking up to the well under the scorching glare of the midday sun. That would be good. I really couldn't ask for more than that. Not me. Not with the stains I carry in my soul.

The man leans forward, looks me straight in the face. "Go, call your husband, and come here."

Oh no.

I swallow. I should not have come to the well today.

"I have no husband." The words wrench from me. I cannot stop them. The truth. As little as I can say, as much as I can manage.

"You are right in saying, 'I have no husband'; for you have had five husbands, and the one you now have is not your husband. What you have said is true."

And there it is. Laid bare. Exposed. All my pain, my shame, the humiliation that is my life. Will I never be free?

Five husbands. Six, really. A number that expresses all that has gone wrong, all that has enslaved me to this life of disgrace. Six, a number twice what the rabbis allow.

And yet, this stranger by the well doesn't sneer when he says it. And he doesn't turn away. He simply speaks the truth. Clear, concise, and without accusation.

I change the topic. "Sir, I perceive that you are a prophet. Our fathers worshiped on this mountain, but you say that in Jerusalem is the place where people ought to worship." There, it is better to talk about politics. Better to throw out something that will get his focus off the one thing I always try to bury, to hide. Six men. Messiahs and mountains are safer than those.

He answers my questions, but I know he's not fooled. He talks of the Messiah, of worshiping in spirit and in truth.

I sigh. "I know that Messiah is coming." The one who is called Christ. "When he comes, he will tell us all things."

"I who speak to you am he."

Could it be? Could *he* be the One?

Could the Messiah we have waited for speak to me, a Samaritan woman who has had six men? Somehow, he knew. He knew just who I was, just what I hid.

And yet, he chose to encounter me at the well in the heat of the day.

Footsteps sound along the path behind me. The men who had passed me by on the road are returning. They gape, but they say nothing to me, nothing to him.

I drop my jar, my emptiness, beside the well and hurry toward town.

I am no longer afraid, no longer ashamed. I will tell the townspeople everything. And I will lead with the one thing I have most wanted to hide. I, who go to the well at noon so the women won't comment on my dishonor. I, who've had more men than I want to count. I, who have carried this pain, this shame, this stain, for longer than I can remember—I will tell my story. "Come!" I will say. "See a man who told me all that I ever did. Can this be the Christ?"

Somehow, in this encounter with a man by the well, my shame has been transformed. I carry it no longer. I thirst no more. And I am filled with wonder.

Shamed

Five husbands. And the one she had now had not even offered the dignity of marriage. Could the husbands have died? Unlikely. This woman is never called a widow. Might she have been a serial adulteress? Perhaps. But Jesus doesn't mention that. He only points out the barest facts of her circumstances, as if he is not interested in who was to blame for her multiple marriages or the fact that she currently lived with a man who was not her husband at all. However, what we can surmise is that this woman was, for reasons unknown, set aside by five men. In her culture, she would not have had a choice to divorce. Only men could write certificates of divorce and send their wives away. And that is the level of brokenness that this woman carried to a well in the heat of the day. That is the level of brokenness that Jesus encountered and sought to heal.

Through the story of this Samaritan woman at the well, Jesus offers us the freedom of grace and truth. He invites us to acknowledge all the betrayals, the hurts, the crushed dreams, the injustices, the pain and the shame, and then to choose life, to drink deeply from the well of living water. This is how we are to be made new. The Samaritan woman leads the way.

In the Heat of the Day

What a mess! That's what I think when I read the story of the Samaritan woman's life. It's not neat. It's not tidy. And it's nothing like what would have been acceptable in her day. Her tragic and scandalous history of broken relationships was a toxic cloud of shame that followed her everywhere. No wonder she didn't go to draw water in the morning with all the other women, as was the custom in villages in Jesus's time, and still is the custom in many villages around the world today.

But on that day, the woman wasn't alone at the well. A stranger waited. A man, and a Jew. It was bad enough that she was a Samaritan. Jewish disdain for Samaritans went back over seven centuries, back to the time the ten northern tribes of Israel were conquered by Assyria, creating a mixed race of Jew and Gentile (2 Kings 17). It certainly didn't help matters that she was a woman. Jewish men were not allowed to talk to women. "It is forbidden to give a woman any greeting," read one rabbinic rule of the day. Another was, "One should not talk with a woman on the street, not even with his own wife."[1]

Still worse, she'd had five husbands, when the rabbis had determined that three was the upper limit for decency.[2] And the man she was living with now apparently didn't respect her enough to marry her.

Her life was a mess. No little Samaritan girl could have imagined her life might turn out as this woman's had—that she would be repeatedly cast off and that her only option for survival would be living with a man who refused her the dignity of marriage. Widowhood would have garnered compassion. But shame came when husbands wrote a certificate of divorce and sent their wives away. For that to happen once was humiliating enough. But probably five times? That was this woman's life, that was the shame she carried with her to the well at noon, when everyone else should have been long gone.

But Jesus waited for her there. He didn't go to the well in the morning either. Nor did he bypass Samaria, as did most of the Jews of the day. Instead, he travelled to Sychar, sat at the well in the heat of the day, and waited for a woman whose life had been scorched by shame.

Jesus meets us in the heat of our shame, too. He doesn't walk around it; he doesn't wait in the cool of what's normal and expected; he doesn't get up and walk away when the sun beats down and the dust of our pain swirls around us. And he doesn't fall for our self-protective distractions, when all we want to do is redirect attention away from the thing that hurts the most.

Jesus doesn't meet us in the pretending or the distractions. He meets us at high noon, in the scorching heat of shame, when everything is all wrong and we can't avoid the truth any longer.

And there, he asks us to face that truth, and to allow his living water to drench the flames of our shame-scorched soul.

Facing Shame

Jesus first asks the Samaritan woman for a drink of water. In doing so, he asks her to engage with him, to look at him, to see him, and choose to interact with him. He asks the same of us. In the heat of those deep, hurting places within us, he invites us to acknowledge him, even if it's only to ask why the God of all the universe would bother to speak to us in our shame.

Jesus then talks about living water, about the gift he has for not only the Samaritan woman, but for all of us—a deep quenching of the thirst in our parched souls. Do you thirst for love? Hope? Healing? A renewal of your dreams? Jesus is living water that cleanses, restores, and gives new life. He satisfies the thirst of our souls.

And yet, we cannot receive that water until we come out of hiding and acknowledge the truth of our shame. "Give me this water," the woman says.

But Jesus doesn't give it immediately. Instead he says, "Go, call your husband."

She would like to soften her shame. "I have no husband," she says.

Jesus could have left it at that, but he doesn't. Instead, he affirms her honesty and then lays out her whole story. "You are right in saying, 'I have no husband,'" he says, "for you have had five husbands, and the one you now have is not your husband. What you have said is true." In commenting on this exchange, author Michael Card writes, "As gently as a doctor unwraps a wound to examine it, Jesus takes the cover off her life. The wounds are deep: there were five slashes of woundedness, and even now there is an ongoing injury because she lives with a man whose love cannot embrace her as his wife. She is discovered—uncovered."[3]

Jesus doesn't ignore her shame. He doesn't discount it or disregard it. He simply states the truth of it, and in so doing, conquers it.

After her encounter with Christ, this woman who endured the heat of the day, most likely to avoid encountering anyone, went directly to the very townspeople she had once sought to evade. And the first words out of her mouth were, "Come, see a man who told me all that I ever did" (John 4:29). She led with the very thing—"all that I ever did"—she had most wanted to hide. It's an amazing transformation!

Jesus transformed her shame into her testimony. He took what was hurtful and ugly and hidden and made it into a thing of wonder that brought others running to him. And the woman didn't have to hide anymore. She didn't have to pretend. She didn't have to sneak to the well when no one was looking.

Jesus longs to meet us, to speak the truth to us, to set us free from shame. "I am the way, and the truth, and the life" he says, "and you will know the truth, and the truth will set you free" (John 14:6; 8:32).

Forever Freed

God offers us the gift of *aletheia*, the Greek word for truth. It derives from a root word meaning "unhidden." Speaking the truth means we don't have to hide anymore. It means we don't have to be ashamed.

Jesus offers us a way to drink deeply of living water. All we need to do is bring our empty jar to the well, where he waits for us in the heat of pain and shame. There, he invites us to acknowledge the truth—all the mess, all the mistakes, all the things we'd like to deny ever happened. There is no shame in the truth, only freedom.

Then, like the Samaritan woman, we can leave our empty jars behind and embrace a transformed life that points not to our shame but to the One who freed us. A life that points others to Jesus and says, "Come and see!"

Who Is God When We're Shamed?

"Come to me, all you who are weary and burdened," Jesus says. "Come to me . . . and I will give you rest" (Matthew 11:28 NIV). And when we accept his invitation, he renews us and begins the process of making us whole. It's a truth we witness again and again throughout the pages of Scripture. Consider just a few examples:

- Mary Magdalene came to Jesus and was freed from seven demons. (Luke 8)
- A man approached Jesus, pleading, "If you are willing, you can make me clean," and Jesus was willing. The man was made clean. (Mark 1)
- A demon-possessed man came to Jesus and was restored to his right mind. (Mark 5)
- A woman who had suffered twelve years of bleeding touched the edge of Jesus's cloak and was not only healed, but also called "daughter" and restored to her place in the community. (Matthew 9)
- A fearful father knelt before Jesus, pleading for mercy, and Jesus healed his son instantly. (Matthew 17)
- A Syrophoenician mother fell at Jesus's feet, persistent in begging for whatever crumbs of compassion he might

offer. He healed her daughter and commended her faith. (Mark 7)

Whatever our condition, Jesus invites us to come. To drink the living water that we may be set free to worship in the Spirit and in truth.

We may not have had a choice in what's happened to us. But we do have a choice whether or not to carry the shame and stain, whether or not to hide it or to come and leave it at the feet of Christ.

Jesus calls you to come to him and live as a woman who is no longer afraid, no longer ashamed. A woman of honor, joy, and bold faith in the One who loves her and sets her free.

> God's light is tender, not harsh. As you trust him with your pain, he will gently shine his healing light on all your wounds. He is for you, not against you—and will never shame you or humiliate you (Romans 8:31).
>
> Christine Caine, *Unashamed*

12

A SINFUL WOMAN
Scorned

Luke 7

Her sins, which are many, are forgiven—for she loved much. But he who is forgiven little, loves little. (Luke 7:44–47)

Scorned. It is to be mocked. Treated with contempt, derision, disdain. It happens all too often in our culture. Women are openly disrespected because of something in their past. Somehow, they are not good enough, clean enough, perfect enough to be valued. And when they don't live up to a standard set by someone else, they are scorned.

— • • • —

I will never forget the day I sat next to my friend at a Christian writers conference and listened as she was told that since she had divorced her husband, she no longer had credibility in the Christian market. The one pronouncing this decree had no idea of the circumstances leading to the divorce. Was there abuse? Infidelity? Verbal battering? It didn't matter. Her previous books had won awards and she had consistently used her writing and communication gifts to lift up the name of Christ, but that didn't matter either. My friend was now a divorced woman and therefore permanently disgraced, according to her accuser, and that was that. She was no longer fit for ministry in the kingdom of God. She was less-than, unworthy, untouchable by Christian publishers.

My mouth gaped as I processed the arrogance behind this dismissive proclamation. It was particularly shocking since two tables away sat a divorced and remarried man who held a high position in one of the Christian publishing companies represented there. My friend's accuser didn't seem to care one whit about that man's past, but felt quite self-assured declaring my friend's unfitness for Christian service.

How poorly we sometimes reflect the grace and love of God when dealing with those who have fallen from our own ideals of respectability! I wonder what Jesus would say to us in our scorn for those who may be forgiven but who we still consider damaged goods. Fortunately, I don't have to wonder very long. To know what he might say, I need only to look to the story of a woman who anointed Jesus's feet with perfume, wept, and wiped his feet with her hair. A woman the religious leaders, and most of the subheadings in our Bibles, label "a sinful woman."

He should know what sort of woman is touching him, thought the Pharisee. *She is a sinner!*

And Jesus did know. She was the sort of woman who loved Jesus enough to ignore the scorn and give everything she had to honor him. She was the sort of woman Jesus praised.

I'm happy to say that my friend didn't allow the comments of her accuser to stop her from serving Jesus either. She didn't stop writing. She didn't give up. Instead, she continued to pour out everything she had to honor Christ through her writing and through her life. I think the woman who knelt at Jesus's feet would approve of my friend's choices. And if we listen carefully, she might tell her story and invite us to kneel there with her . . .

A SINFUL WOMAN SPEAKS OUT

My heart almost stops when I see him. Normally, I scurry past the house of Simon, the Pharisee. But this time, I pause. I look again. It is Jesus, the rabbi from Nazareth, the one whose words have changed my life. Changed me. He reclines at the table tucked just inside a large room attached to the courtyard. The doors are open wide, as is the custom. He has only just started the meal.

I catch my breath. If I hurry . . .

I lift my skirts an inch off the ground and dash home. It is not very decorous, but it doesn't matter, no one expects decorum from me. Everyone knows what I am.

I reach my room and grab my most prized possession, an alabaster flask of perfumed ointment. It is worth three hundred denarii, a princely sum. I've been saving it most of my life. I won't save it any longer.

I rush back to Simon's house and enter the courtyard. The Master's feet stretch out behind him at the table. I don't hesitate but walk quickly to kneel behind him. I am so close to him. So close to the One who has set my heart free.

And suddenly, I am weeping with a mix of sorrow, joy, and gratitude I cannot contain. My tears fall on the dust of his feet, making wet rivulets across his skin. I feel the scornful stare of the Pharisee as his gaze bores into me.

But I don't care.

I am near Jesus. How can I care what Simon and others think?

I unbind my hair. The rabbis say it is indecent for a woman to unbind her hair in front of any but her husband.

I don't care.

Jesus is here.

I weep and wipe his feet with my hair. I kiss his feet. My hands shake as I draw out my alabaster jar. It is all I have. All that I own of any worth. I break it and anoint his feet with the ointment. A pure, sweet scent fills the room.

I glance up, breathing in the heady fragrance. Simon's gaze slides from me to the Master. His face hardens with judgment. He knows I am a sinner. The whole town knows. Will he rebuke me? Will he rebuke the man who set me free from my life of sin? Will he dare?

Jesus doesn't give him the chance. "Simon, I have something to say to you," he says.

Simon's voice is cold as he answers. "Say it, Teacher."

And through my tears and the welling of love in my soul, I hear Jesus tell a story of moneylenders, debtors, and love.

Love.

Jesus looks at Simon but motions toward me with his hand. "Do you see this woman?"

Simon's eyes still blaze with scorn as he looks at me. I spare him less than a moment's glance, because now, my gaze is fixed on the One I love. I see only him. I hear only him. And I kiss his feet again.

Jesus speaks once more to Simon, but now his eyes are on me. Eyes filled not with scorn but with deep love and compassion. "I entered your house; you gave me no water for my feet, but she has wet my feet with her tears and wiped them with her hair. You gave me no kiss, but from the time I came in she has not ceased to kiss my feet. You did not anoint my head with oil, but she has anointed my feet with ointment. Therefore I tell you, her sins, which are many, are forgiven—for she loved much. But he who is forgiven little, loves little."

Then he smiles at me. "Your sins are forgiven."

I know. Somehow, I know. There is such freedom in me, such joy, that I can barely contain it.

"Your faith has saved you," he says. "Go in peace."

Peace. Forgiveness. Salvation.

All this he offers freely to me, a woman weeping at his feet. The scorn of the Pharisee and the townspeople no longer matter to me. All that matters is Jesus. All that matters is that he doesn't condemn. He has set me free.

I close my eyes and allow the scent of the ointment to surround me. I have held nothing back. I poured out everything I had, the whole jar, at his feet. And I am filled with an unspeakable joy.

Scorned

Perhaps you understand what it's like to be scorned because of something in your past. You have felt the sting when other Christians, even leaders in the church, treat you as less-than, as damaged, as unworthy. Perhaps you have been excluded, given sidelong glances of disapproval, whispered about behind your back. Maybe you've even been deemed unfit.

If so, I invite you to come alongside a weeping woman with a broken alabaster jar and to kneel with her at Jesus's feet. I'll kneel there with you. And together we'll glimpse the heart of Christ for those who are scorned and see his redemption for those who are shunned.

What Matters?

She was known only as a "sinful woman." She has no name, no identity, no story. Why was she sinful? Why did the town scorn her? What had she done?

We don't know. The text is silent on why she is considered a sinful woman, though scholars and commentators like to speculate. Perhaps she was a prostitute or an adulteress. Perhaps she was sexually promiscuous (commentators always seem to point to sexual sin first). But we don't know. For all we know, she could have been a habitual liar, a petty thief, or a gossip. Or, as New Testament scholar David E. Garland points out, she may simply have been married to a notorious sinner.[1]

Why doesn't the text clarify?

We can't know that for sure either. But I think it might be because the nature of her sins, which Jesus says are "many," doesn't matter. It never has. Consider, for example, a few other people the Bible describes as forgiven:

- Simon Peter falls down at Jesus's knees and cries out, "Depart from me, for I am a sinful man, O Lord" (Luke 5:8), and yet Jesus called him to be a disciple, an evangelist, a missionary, a pastor and—even after Peter denied Jesus three times—a key leader in the early church.

- The prophet Isaiah says, "Woe is me! For I am lost; for I am a man of unclean lips, and I dwell in the midst of a people of unclean lips" (Isaiah 6:5), and yet God commissioned him to prophesy to the nation of Israel and bring God's word to the people.

- Rahab was a prostitute in Jericho, yet she saved the Israelite spies and became an ancestor in the line of Jesus.

- And of course, there's Mary Magdalene, from whom seven demons were cast out, who became one of the women who accompanied Jesus and the disciples and "provided for them out of their means" (Luke 8:3), and was the first to see Jesus after his resurrection.

Did Rahab's former prostitution define her, make her worthy of scorn? Not at all! Her faith defined her—that's what mattered. Did Peter's denial of Christ mean he should be rejected and shunned? Of course not! He was a prominent leader of the church after Jesus's death and resurrection. And Mary who had been demon-possessed? She's best known today for her devotion to Jesus. God not only forgave these people, he subsequently called and commissioned them to do his work.

Similarly, in our passage, Jesus's interactions with a sinful woman give us a lesson on love. We don't need to know her sin. To Jesus, it was her demonstration of love that mattered most.

However, it's important to note that Jesus didn't excuse her sin or overlook it. He didn't say her sinning did not matter. He doesn't say all she needs is love. Instead of scorning her for sin, Jesus forgives her. Sets her free. Makes her clean. And we can surmise that whatever her sin was, it was over and in her past. If not, Jesus would have said, as he did on other occasions, "Go and sin no more." Instead, he said simply, "Go in peace."

Jesus doesn't define the woman by her sin. Her sin, however, is all Simon the Pharisee can see. He who is supposed to represent the best of their faith could see nothing but a sinful woman. "If this man were a prophet, he would have known what sort of woman this is who is touching him," Simon thinks. As readers, we can't help but hear the sneer in his thoughts. The scorn. The contempt and disdain.

But in the face of the Pharisee's derision, Jesus praises the woman. He lifts her up as a model for the foolish Pharisee to follow.

Simon gave Jesus no water. The woman cleaned God's feet with her tears and hair.

Simon gave Jesus no kiss. The woman lavished kisses on the feet of God.

Simon did not anoint Jesus's head. The woman poured expensive ointment all over God's feet.

And she did it all while the scornful, judging eyes of the Pharisee were fixed on her. She did it while she was being disparaged and despised.

Take a moment to think about that. She was so focused on Jesus that it didn't matter what the Pharisee thought or said. She just kept pouring out her gratitude and love.

Who wins? The critical judge who thought himself pure and blameless? Or a sinful woman who chose to love anyway? Her sins were forgiven. Simon's were not.

And who loses? Not the woman; she was praised and blessed by Jesus. But Simon? He had Jesus in his own home. At his very own table! He had every opportunity to love and learn. To be near the incarnate God. Instead, he chose condemnation for the woman, and for Jesus. And when Jesus speaks, Simon is clearly the one who comes out on the bottom. He had no benefit from Jesus at all. His opinion didn't matter at all. The woman was praised, her sins forgiven. She was set free. She was blessed by the words, "Go in peace."

So what matters most to you—the sin you've committed or the love you've shown? What people, even leaders in the church, say about you? Or Jesus, who forgives and frees you?

Are you consumed by what's been done to you in the past? Do your experiences of betrayal, abuse, degradation, harassment define you?

Hear the words of Jesus as he says, "Your sins are forgiven. Go in peace." Your pain doesn't have to define you. We are all sinners. We all have things in our past we wish had never happened. But what Jesus offers us is not scorn; it's not condemnation. Rather, he calls us to faith, love, hope.

Jesus saves you. You are invited by him to live in peace. To live in love.

If we choose to accept his invitation, then what is the next step? How do we live in the truth of our healing and freedom?

Who Do You Listen To?

There's an interesting dynamic of shame and blame, of scorn, that sometimes happens in my household of six kids. Today, it played out in an exchange between my thirteen-year-old daughter Bria and my ten-year-old son Jayden. It went something like this:

Bria: Jayden didn't put his plate in the dishwasher.

Jayden: Bria! I did too.

Me: Bria, that's Jayna's plate. Jayden cleaned up after himself.

Jayden to Bria (with increasing volume): I did too, Bria! Stop trying to make me look bad.

Me: Jayden did what he was told.

Bria to Jayden: You never put your dishes away.

Me: He did this time.

Jayden (still totally ignoring me): I do too. I put my plate away. Stop being mean, Bria!

Me: (Heaves a big sigh.)

You would think that Jayden would be satisfied that I was backing him up, especially since I was the authority in that situation. You'd think he'd rest in my praise and affirmation of his innocence. But no. All it takes is one sibling saying something critical or negative about another, and that becomes the only thing the criticized one can hear.

Thank goodness the woman with the alabaster jar wasn't like that! She knew who to listen to: Jesus. She focused exclusively on him. In fact, she did not cease kissing Jesus's feet even when others were talking about her. She heard only Jesus, paid attention only to him.

I want to be like that—so focused on gratitude and love that I have no room to dwell on the scorn of the Pharisees in my life. I never want to allow the critics to distract me from showing love to God or from following his will for me.

The key, I believe, is firmly deciding whose opinion matters. Do we care about the scornful comments of those who are mean-spirited and judgmental? Do we let them pull us away from Jesus's feet? What if they're religious leaders? Simon was! His opinion was supposed to matter . . . or was it?

In comparison to the opinion of Jesus, Simon's opinion meant nothing at all. And that's how it should be. If those around us, even leaders in the church, degrade and deride us, then they are not showing the character of Jesus. Jesus says we are forgiven. Jesus says we are made new. He is the one who offers freedom and peace. He is the one who calls us to come near.

The Whole Jar

What if we could truly live our lives as the woman in the story lived that moment at Jesus's feet? Is such a thing possible? Can we imagine living each day as if all that mattered to us was Jesus's love for us and our love for him? What if we were so taken, so entranced, so overcome with the wonder of his love, what if we were so focused on pouring out the whole of who we are, that we didn't even pay attention to the negativity of anyone else? What wonder, what joy, what freedom would fill our lives!

This woman came to Jesus with nothing, and she came with all she had. Her tears, her sorrow, her pain, and her one possession—an alabaster jar of costly ointment. She unbound her hair, a thing a woman was only supposed to do in front her spouse. She came with her humility and humiliation and dried his feet. She came with her past, her reputation as a sinful woman. And she came with her future, symbolized in the alabaster jar that was likely her life savings and security. And she poured out both her past and her future at his feet.

She came with no expectations, no judgment, no self-righteousness, and no self-condemnation. She came with no reservations, and she poured out the whole of who she was for Jesus.

Do we really want to do anything less?

When others criticize and condemn, what if we didn't even look up but kept our focus on loving Jesus? When others scorn us, talk behind our backs, what if we chose instead to hear only what Jesus says of us? What if we lay everything we have and everything we are, the good and the bad, at the feet of Jesus and trust him to speak to our souls?

I want to leave everything at Jesus's feet. Jesus stands up for me and for you, and he says, "Your sins are forgiven. . . . Go in peace."

Who Is God When We're Scorned?

God's preference for the scorned or the overlooked is a pattern evident throughout biblical history.

- From the very beginning, God repeatedly chose to honor second sons, such as Abel, Jacob, Ephraim, over their older brothers. Culture said the firstborn son was the most important, the heir, the one who would inherit not only the father's land, but also the father's (and therefore God's) blessing. And yet, God almost always ignored societal hierarchies to give a special place to the overlooked second son. Even Moses was a second son. Our position in life's pecking order isn't what matters to God.

- When Jacob was chosen over Esau as the heir of God's covenant, God chose the scorned, unloved, supposedly unattractive wife, Leah, not the beloved and beautiful Rachel, for the lineage of Jesus. How valuable, pretty, or loveable others think we are doesn't matter. God's love matters. He loved Leah. And he loves you.

- When it came time to choose a king after God's own heart, God chose David. David was not only the youngest, but he was also the smallest of his brothers. His lack of brawn and height would have seemed to disqualify him as a potential leader. Yet God chose him to be king of Israel, to the surprise of both his father and Samuel the prophet. *Surely not him!* they thought. But he was the one chosen, and the one who loved God all his life. Love for God matters more than what we look like.

- When God chose to become a human being and dwell among us, he chose a mere girl from the despised town of Nazareth to be the one who bore him. Where you come from doesn't matter. God sees the heart.

- Jesus picked mere fishermen from Galilee to be his closest friends. These were not fancy Pharisees, not leaders from the capital of Jerusalem, not men of royalty or influence but lowly fishermen! And a despised tax collector, the most scorned of occupations. And, wonder of wonders, a greedy guy who ended up stealing from their moneybag! Our willingness to leave everything and follow Jesus matters much more than our pedigree, our occupation, or even our ability to love well! Sadly, for Judas, in the end he chose not to love at all. But Jesus gave him every opportunity. Jesus called him anyway, loved him anyway, included him anyway.

- And of course, there's Jesus himself. He came not as a rich and powerful king, but as a babe born in a barn and laid in a feeding trough. His family was so poor they could afford only two doves or two young pigeons for his presentation at the temple when he was eight days old. There was no fattened calf for him! Throughout his ministry, he was scorned, humiliated, disdained. Nathanael said of him, "Can anything good come out of Nazareth?" (John 1:46).

A psalm that Jesus quoted described himself: "The stone that the builders rejected has become the cornerstone" (Luke 20:17). Jesus was rejected, scorned, sneered at, derided and debased. He died from it. And then he rose from the dead and redeemed all the rejection, scorn, derision, and disdain—for you, for me. For us all.

Have the builders rejected you? Let Jesus build you into a temple to the living God. Have others scorned you? Focus only on Jesus and his words to you—*go in peace*. Have those you trusted looked down on you? Kneel at the feet of Jesus and pour out your love to him.

That's all that really matters.

> Blessed is she who has believed that the Lord would fulfill his promises to her!
>
> Luke 1:45 (NIV)

13

A WOMAN CAUGHT IN ADULTERY

Blamed

John 8:1–11

And Jesus said, "Neither do I condemn you; go, and from now on sin no more." (John 8:11)

———— • • • ————

B lamed. Held responsible. Sometimes, solely responsible for a wrong that requires two people. Blame, is a nasty, insidious thing. There is a sinister power to it that suppresses real justice and prevents real healing.

———— • • • ————

It was the first day of my senior year in high school. I'd been away most of the summer attending special college courses for high school students at Harvard University. So, strolling into the cafeteria that first day felt like a journey into a now-foreign world. My gaze swept across the room, looking for familiar faces. There, at the far end of a long table sat one of my closest friends. I smiled and strode over to her, eager to catch up on the summer happenings.

She glanced up as I plopped into the seat next to her. "So, how was your summer?"

Her face hardened. "It was okay."

I frowned. "What happened? I haven't heard anything."

She sighed as her eyes darted around the room. Her gaze landed on a boy three tables over. Then she looked away.

"Isn't that the guy you were interested in?" I asked.

For a moment she didn't answer, which meant the answer was yes. And no. And . . .

"What happened?"

She took a deep breath and answered quickly, in monotone. "He found out I liked him and invited me to a party. I went with him. We were having a good time. I thought he liked me. Then he slipped something into my drink and . . ." Her lips clamped shut.

My heart thudded. "Oh, no. Did he—"

"Yes."

"Did you tell the police?"

She shook her head. "Nobody believed me. And those who did said it was my fault anyway. They knew I liked him, and so, well . . . you know."

I didn't know. I didn't want to know. I wanted to believe in justice. I wanted to believe that guys didn't just get away with date rape and go about their lives as if nothing had happened, while the girl was left to pick up the pieces of her life. And yet, there was the perpetrator, sitting a few tables over, laughing with his friends, enjoying the first day of his senior year.

"Don't look at him. I don't want anyone to know I'm talking about him."

I looked away. My fists clenched. I wanted to scream. I wanted to hug her. I wanted to cry. I wanted to march over and punch him in the face. And drag him to the principal. And demand justice. And . . .

She put her hand on my arm. "I know. It's no use, though. Everyone will just point fingers at me."

I blinked away my tears. She didn't want me to make a scene in the school cafeteria. But oh, I wish I had been there for her at that party. I wish I knew what to say. I wish I knew a way to make things better when she bore the burden of another's crimes and the criminal got off scot-free.

But I was just a seventeen-year-old girl at a time when people didn't talk about these things, and authorities often blamed the victim because "she was asking for it." There is power in blame. It can threaten, it can oppress, it can propagate gross injustice.

My friend believed that she would be accused, and just the threat of it ignited in her a fear strong enough to let that boy get away with his crime, no questions asked. He got off scot-free, just like the man who is nowhere to be found in the New Testament story of the woman caught in adultery.

My friend's story may seem a strange one to connect to the story of the woman caught in adultery. After all, my friend was date raped and this woman had been complicit in adultery. A story of a modern woman blamed for an affair would seem to be a better fit. Perhaps. But even though the circumstances are different, when I think of the power of blame to shame and to silence, it is my friend's face that shimmers before my mind's eye. And somehow, it reflects the face of the woman standing silently before Jesus as others clutch their condemnation in the form of stones about to be thrown.

So as we turn to the woman caught in adultery, I wonder what she might say to other victims of the blame game. Might she offer hope to those for whom blame has become the great unequalizer and silencer of justice? What wisdom, what insights, what comfort might we gain from her unusual encounter with a rabbi who wrote in the dirt? Perhaps she would have told her story something like this . . .

A WOMAN CAUGHT IN ADULTERY SPEAKS OUT

The air tastes like dust in my mouth. Dry. Filthy. Deadly. I close my eyes to the smug faces around me. They caught me. In his bed. In my sin. No excuses. Early in the morning.

They caught him, too. But he wasn't here with me now. He walked away. Snuck away, uncondemned. And they looked the other way when he did. It is only me being dragged to the temple for judgment. Only me being pushed, shoved toward my doom. I open my eyes.

I know the law. I know the penalty for adultery is death by stoning. Even now, some carry rocks in their fists. I shiver.

The morning sun throws a shard of light across the temple courts, and I see a man sitting, with a crowd already gathered around him. A rabbi, teaching.

Rough hands shove me toward the man and the feet of my accusers pick up speed as we approach. The rabbi continues to teach, his gaze wandering the crowd in front of him as he speaks. He does not look at me. He does not look at the religious leaders who thrust me forward until I stand in the center of the crowd. Until I stand before the rabbi in the temple courts.

"Teacher!" One of the Pharisees steps beside me, his voice a sneer in my ears. "This woman has been caught in the act of adultery."

And there it is. The words that spell my death. I stand before them all, silent, as I bear the consequences. Alone.

The rabbi turns toward us. Then he stands. His gaze betrays nothing. Calm. Impassive. Waiting.

We both wait.

A scribe continues, his tone pious and cruel. "Now in the Law, Moses commanded us to stone such women. So what do you say?"

What would he say?

I wait.

Instead of speaking, the rabbi bends down and writes with his finger on the ground. He writes! And I cannot see the words that draw his attention to the dust at our feet.

Those who brought me continue to badger him. *What do you say? Do you condemn her? What's your judgment, Teacher?* They use his title as a jeer. If they do not respect his judgment, why did they bring me before him?

Several in the circle of men around me pick up rocks, ready to stone me at the rabbi's command. Would he tell them to let the stones fly?

He should. Everyone knew the law. I knew it. But the law said that we should *both* be stoned—the woman and the man. Both who were caught in adultery should be punished.

And yet I stand in the middle of a circle of stones, bearing the blame alone.

"Render your judgment," a Pharisee demands.

I shudder as the rabbi stands and turns to the crowd. How many rocks will it take to kill me? How many blows before my life ends? How many before my sentence is executed and his, the man I was with, not even begun?

Unfair. Unjust. But nobody cares about justice for a woman like me.

Then, the rabbi renders judgment. "Let him who is without sin among you be the first to throw a stone at her."

My gaze snaps to him, then to the crowd around me.

But he is not looking at me. He simply stoops again and writes mysteries in the sand.

One by one, my accusers drop their stones. From the oldest to the youngest. One by one, they turn. One by one, they leave me.

I swallow and wait. Amazed.

Then, it is just the two of us. I stand alone with the man who writes in the dust.

He stands and looks at me for a long moment. "Woman, where are they? Has no one condemned you?"

I want to laugh. I want to cry. I thought I was alone, but he was with me. And now, there are no accusers left. All the stones have fallen.

"No one, Lord." No one. Lord. My Lord. The only one who matters.

He smiles at me and nods. "Neither do I condemn you." And in those words, I know he is the only one who could condemn—and he chooses not to. "Go, and from now on sin no more."

I tremble. I stood condemned. Filled with shame and sin. And now, he has freed me.

Who is this who forgives my sin? Who is this who stands with me in the center of a circle of stones and declares not my condemnation but my freedom? Who is this whose power is greater than the power of blame?

Who is this rabbi who has set me free not only from death but from my stain?

I will go and sin no more. I turn with a fierce gladness to a new way, a new life.

It isn't fair. It isn't just. I came here alone. The only one caught. The only one accused. The only one condemned.

And yet, I also leave alone. The only one freed. The only one forgiven. The only one made new by this rabbi who writes in the dust.

I glance back. A breeze blows away the dust of his scribbles. His eyes are on me. And it hits me full force—what they intended for my harm, he has used for my good.

I was caught. I was accused and condemned. And yet, I received an unimaginable blessing.

And the man I was with in bed this morning? He did not.

I catch my breath. Who is this rabbi, this man, this Lord, who changes injustice into mercy? Who conquers blame and turns it to blessing?

Who is this who takes wrong and makes it more than right?

Blamed

Scholars consider the story found in John 8:1–11 a "textual floater," which means that it's not clear exactly where the story was originally placed in the Gospels. In fact, it's not included in the earliest manuscripts of John. In a few of the later manuscripts, it's found in Luke. Eventually, it found its permanent home at the beginning of John 8, where it fits best with John's themes focusing on disputes with the Pharisees and the identity and authority of the Messiah.

Augustine of Hippo (AD 354–430), a theologian who often fixated on the morality (or lack thereof) of women, had his own theory. He argued that this story had actually been removed from the earlier manuscripts so as not to encourage the sin of adultery in women. In other words, in his view, women were so morally depraved that a story of God's grace and forgiveness would surely tempt them to sin. Therefore, it had been removed from the biblical text. He nowhere mentioned, or even seemed to consider, whether the absence of the man would tempt men to think they could sin and get away with it.

Really? Doesn't the very nature of adultery require two people, a man and a woman? But in this story, the man is absent. Why was only the woman brought before Jesus? If she was "caught in the act of adultery" as the passage claims, then the man ought to have been caught as well. He too should have borne the consequences according to the law: "If a man commits adultery with the wife of his neighbor, both the adulterer and the adulteress shall surely be put to death" (Leviticus 20:10).

Did they believe only the woman was to blame?

It's the Woman's Fault?

The church has a disgraceful record when it comes to blaming women for the sins of men. Here is a brief sampling of statements made about women by leaders from the earliest days of the church:

- "Woman, you are the gate to hell." Tertullian (ca. AD 155–ca. 222), known as the father of Latin Christianity, *De Cultu Feminarum* (On the Apparel of Women)

- "[Women's] very consciousness of their own nature must evoke feelings of shame." Clement of Alexandria (AD 150–215), Christian theologian, *Pedagogues II*

- "What is the difference whether it is in a wife or a mother, it is still Eve the temptress that we must beware of in any woman. . . . I fail to see what use woman can be to man, if one excludes the function of bearing children." Augustine (354–430), Bishop of Hippo, *De Genesi ad litteram—Libri Duodecim* (The Literal Meaning of Genesis in Twelve Books)

- "Woman is a misbegotten man and has a faulty and defective nature in comparison to his. Therefore she is unsure in herself. What she cannot get, she seeks to obtain through lying and diabolical deceptions. And so, to put it briefly, one must be on one's guard with every woman, as if she were a poisonous snake and the horned devil. . . . Thus in evil and perverse doings woman is cleverer, that is, slyer, than man. Her feelings drive woman toward every evil, just as reason impels man toward all good." Albertus Magnus (1205–1280), German Dominican theologian, *Quaestiones super de animalibus* (Questions Concerning Aristotle's *On Animals*)

- "For if there be not fear and reverence in the inferior [women], there can be no sound nor constant honor yielded to the superior [men]." John Dod (1549–1645), *A Plaine and Familiar Exposition of the Tenne Commandements*, a Puritan guidebook published in 1603

- "The Holiness of God is not evidenced in women when they are brash, brassy, boisterous, brazen, head-strong, strong-willed, loud-mouthed, overly-talkative, having to have the last word, challenging, controlling, manipulative, critical, conceited, arrogant, aggressive, assertive, strident, interruptive, undisciplined, insubordinate, disruptive, dominating, domineering, or clamoring for power. Rather, women accept God's holy order and character by being humbly and unobtrusively respectful and receptive in functional subordination to God, church leadership, and husbands." James Fowler (1940–2015), American theologian, professor, and pastor, "Women in

the Church," an outline and commentary on 1 Timothy
2:9–15, dated 1999

- "The feminist agenda is not about equal rights for
women. It is about a socialist, anti-family political movement that encourages women to leave their husbands,
kill their children, practice witchcraft, destroy capitalism
and become lesbians." Pat Robertson (1930–), American
televangelist and former Southern Baptist minister, written in a 1992 fundraising letter

These are but a small sample that demonstrate how the
pervasive culture and belief throughout church history has
been that women are so inherently flawed that they must be
subdued through subjugation to men. Otherwise, they will
perpetuate evil in every imaginable form, including but not
limited to sexual promiscuity.

So I suppose we shouldn't be surprised that the Pharisees
blamed only the woman and brought her alone to stand
before Jesus and be stoned. Sexist blame is old. It was preva-
lent in Jesus's culture, in the culture of the early church, and
it continues in our culture today. And yet, the one place we
do not find it is in the actions and attitudes of Jesus, the One
who fully embodies the character of God. In Jesus, there is
not even a hint of sexism. There is nothing—*nothing!*— that
would support the degrading claims made about women
throughout the history of the church.

Which is why reading those quotes makes my jaw tighten
and my heart beat faster. It's not fair!

It's not fair that women are singled out and blamed for sins
for which men are equally responsible. Women are prone to
sexual promiscuity, but men are not? Women are easily tempted
to sin, but men are not? Women are by nature weak, foolish,
and wicked, but men are by nature strong, wise, and holy?

A woman caught in the very act of adultery was dragged to the temple and threatened with stoning, while the man simply slipped away with no condemnation whatsoever? It's not fair! It's not fair that she had to endure judgment alone. It's not fair that they wanted to stone only her. It's not fair that women are still blamed for reprehensible behavior on the part of men because they somehow brought it on themselves.

It's not fair.

Flipping the Script

It's not fair. But for whom?

What if we are looking at the story all wrong? Sure, the man ducks out of the consequences for his sin. The woman bears all the blame. But she also receives all the grace, all the love, all the forgiveness.

Hiddenness isn't freedom. At first glance, we may think the man is free because he has escaped public condemnation and consequences. But what this story makes clear is that what he's really free from is redemption, forgiveness, blessing, and the chance at a new life. He is free from an amazing encounter with Christ.

But this woman dragged before Jesus in attempt to trap the Teacher? She gets it all. She has an encounter with Jesus that changes everything, that changes her. Pause and ponder that for a long moment. Because that is the nature of God—he takes injustice and flips the script. He pours out grace and mercy. That is the power and wonder of our God—what men intended for evil, he uses not just for good but for amazing redemption. For real freedom. For real restoration. For new life.

The man is stuck with his sin. He may not be stoned for it, but the very nature of sin is that of a disease. Sin never goes into remission; it eats away at the flesh, it destroys the soul.

In escaping the consequences of his sin, the man also escapes his healing.

Not so for the woman.

The Pharisees intended to put the whole blame on her. But Jesus, scribbling in the dirt, turns the whole thing back on them and their sin. "Let him who is without sin among you be the first to throw a stone at her" he says (John 8:7). And suddenly, the woman is not the only sinner—because now, everyone is. Sin is an equal opportunity offender. It ensnares all.

And all can be forgiven . . . when we consent to stand alone, exposed, before Jesus rather than hide from the truth of our sin. It is only the woman to whom Jesus says, "Neither do I condemn you," as he bids her to sin no more. It is only the woman who goes home free.

It just wasn't fair . . . for the men in the story! The woman sinned. The men all sinned. And yet only the woman is freed from condemnation.

The woman caught in adultery had sinned, and so she legitimately bore the blame for her part. However, some of us, like my friend from high school, have not sinned but were blamed anyway, accused anyway, condemned anyway.

If Jesus offered forgiveness, wholeness, and healing to the woman caught in adultery, won't he offer it to those who have been blamed for situations in which they had no control, no voice, and so should bear no blame? Just as he did for the woman caught in adultery, Jesus can flip the script today so that the one who is unjustly blamed receives freedom and blessing.

Sexism exists. Prejudice exists. Unfair blame exists. But none of these injustices can keep us from Jesus. In fact, sometimes they can draw us toward him, and when they do, what was meant for our harm can be turned to our everlasting good in the hands of God.

Jesus flips the script. Jesus blesses. Jesus sets free.

The Pharisees did no favors for the man caught in adultery when they allowed him to escape. They simply protected him from forgiveness and healing.

So what might it look like for Jesus to flip the script for you? Have you been burdened with carrying the blame for what was done to you? Have you hidden, like my friend, to avoid the accusing stares and the stones others seem ready to throw?

If so, let us fix our eyes not on the fairness or unfairness of blame, but instead on the One who writes the mysteries of grace and mercy in the sand.

Who Is God When We're Blamed?

All sin and fall short of the glory of God. But only Jesus has the right to cast the first stone. Only he is without sin. And yet, in this story, Jesus stood with the woman as she was surrounded by stones. When the stones dropped, both Jesus and the woman were encircled. And in that circle of stones, Jesus inexplicably stooped down to write in the dirt.

We can't know for sure what Jesus wrote in the sand, though many speculate. For me, the content doesn't matter. Rather, I like what Bede (AD 672–735), an English monk, wrote in his *Homilies on the Gospels*: "[Jesus] desired to write with his finger on the ground, in order to point out that it was he himself who once wrote the Ten Commandments of the law on stone with his finger."[1]

The finger that wrote, "You shall not commit adultery" (Exodus 20:14) on stone tablets was the same finger that now wrote in the sand within a circle of stone.

That is the power of Christ. He makes the stones fall. He rights the wrongs, reverses the injustices, flips the scripts, and opens the way to a new life and a new hope.

God will not rest until he has restored what was broken by our sin, by all of our sin. This God sees you for who you really are and says to you, "Neither do I condemn you; go, and from now on sin no more."

> So in quiet humility and without personal agenda, I make the decision to let God sort it all out. I sit quietly in His presence and simply say, "God, I want Your truth to be the loudest voice in my life. Correct me. Comfort me. Come closer still. And I will trust. God, You are good at being God."
>
> Lysa TerKeurst, *Uninvited*

14

WOMEN AT THE TOMB
Witnesses to Wonder

Luke 24

Now it was Mary Magdalene and Joanna and
Mary the mother of James and the other women
with them who told these things to the apostles.
(Luke 24:10)

It happens all the time in childhood. We revel in climbing
trees and running through sprinklers. We stop to gaze at
daisies and catch our breath at the flight of a butterfly. We
laugh at the scuttling of insects, and even the dirt holds a
hidden glory. In childhood, beauty is not so rare and life is
painted with the vivid colors of awe.

That is wonder. Wonder is found in those moments when
the unexpected glory of God makes us catch our breath. In
those moments, our pain fades before the brilliance of who
God is and the magnitude of his love for us.

Wonder that finds its home in God has the power to restore our souls, to renew our faith, to bind the broken places and make us whole.

————— · · · —————

I walk quietly beside these women of valor and courage from the Old and New Testaments. I close my eyes and listen to the stories they tell. I think and ponder. And as we come now to the end of our journey through the stories of these women of the Bible, as we listen to them speak out, I know I want to be with them one more time.

I want to walk with them in a garden that holds an empty tomb with the stone rolled away. I want to breathe deeply the air of redemption. I want to stand in the sun and peer into the darkness to see the place where they laid my Jesus. And more than that, I want to hear the angels speaking to me. I want to hear the words of incredible hope.

"Why do you look for the living among the dead?"

"He is not here. He has risen!"

"Go, tell the others . . ."

Go, tell them that Jesus is not lying dead and helpless in the tombs of hurt, injustice, abuse, hopelessness, domination, fear, and horror. No, he has risen to overcome the places of death in your life, in mine, and in all our lives. He is alive.

It delights me that the ones whom Jesus entrusted with the most important news of all history were a small group of faithful women. Women like you. Women like me. Mary Magdalene, Joanna, Mary the mother of James, and others who would proclaim the tomb empty, the Lord risen, indeed. Women, together, would be the first witnesses to the wonder and hope of Christ's resurrection.

And perhaps it is time we followed their lead . . .

WOMEN AT THE TOMB SPEAK OUT

Our hands tremble on the jars of spices. It is early, barely dawn. We watched as Joseph from the town of Arimathea took the body of Jesus and laid it in his own tomb. It was almost the Sabbath then, no time for preparing the corpse with spices. Joseph could only wrap Jesus's bloodied body in a fine linen cloth and place him on the low bench. We saw where he was laid and how he was placed. Then, we observed the Sabbath. But now the Sabbath is over and a new day is dawning. Now we come again to the tomb to prepare his body.

But who will roll away the stone? We are all wondering, but nobody asks it aloud. None of us dare to break the silence of the dawn on the third day after his death.

His death.

Guards will be at the tomb. But it is sealed and they will not open it for us. We go anyway. It is our duty, our privilege, our calling. The men are hidden away. They dare not come.

But we dare. Even after Jesus's arrest. Even after his trial. Even after his beating and sentencing. I can still hear the voices screaming, "Crucify him!" I can feel the horror, and the fear. And still we dare.

Even after his crucifixion. And his burial.

One day passed.

Two days passed.

And now, very early on the morning of the third day, we travel to his tomb with burial spices clutched in our hands.

We enter the garden, walk back toward the tomb. Then we stop. The stone has been rolled away. The guards are gone.

We hurry toward the entrance to the tomb and slip inside. It's empty. There are grave cloths where he lay, but there is no body. We look at each other, eyes wide, not knowing whether to be afraid or terrified. Not knowing what to think at all. What to believe.

And then, two men are standing by us, dressed in dazzling apparel. We squint at them, then bow our faces to the ground.

The men speak. "Why do you seek the living among the dead? He is not here, but has risen!"

Risen? Could it be?

"Remember how he told you, while he was still in Galilee, that the Son of Man must be delivered into the hands of sinful men and be crucified and the third day rise."

We did remember. I remembered.

He is risen. He is risen, indeed?

And we, a group of women, are the witnesses to this miracle. This wonder. This resurrection of more than a man. And with him, all our hopes, all his promises, all the possibilities we thought dead and gone.

We must tell the men. We must tell everyone!

We run back to where the men are gathered. We tell them everything. But they don't believe us. Of course they don't. We are but women.

But we are witnesses all the same. And whether or not they believe us, we will tell of this wonder. We will bear witness to the glory.

How could we not, when it was us, the women who love him, who were chosen to be the first at the empty tomb?

Witnesses to Wonder

There is something so beautiful about the fact that women were the first to the tomb, the first witnesses of the resurrection. God knew they would be disbelieved. In their culture, the words and witness of women were not valued. The Jewish historian Josephus (AD 37–100) wrote that due to their giddiness and impetuosity, women were not to be trusted or believed as witnesses for any matter.[1] Imagine, then, how radical it was that women were chosen as the first witnesses to the most important event of human history!

God chose these women to be his first witnesses. Despite their place in society, despite the culture that denied them credibility, despite the lack of trust even from the men in their own community, the angels delivered their message first to women. Jesus chose the women.

He chooses women today, too. When we're used, abused, cast aside, devalued, endangered, dominated, oppressed, shamed, scorned, blamed, and disbelieved, God chooses us too. He chooses you.

You and I, we stand alongside the women who were first to the tomb and we proclaim his glory. You are not "less than" because you are a woman. The women at the tomb assure us of that much. And more. Jesus values you. He calls you to stand up, to live fully in the assurance of his love for you. To be boldly confident in his redemption, his hope, and his healing.

So stand. Stand alongside Eve who witnessed the first stirrings of God's restoration after she and Adam sinned. Stand with Sarah and Hagar to point to a love that sees and redeems. Stand with Lot's daughters and a Levite's concubine and proclaim that women matter. We matter to God.

Stand with two Tamars and Hannah, Abigail and Bathsheba. Stand with Esther and declare that no matter our situation, God gives us choices. Choices to believe, to trust him, to do what is right. To make a positive difference in our world.

Stand with Mary and Martha, a Samaritan woman, a sinful woman, and a woman caught in adultery. Affirm that

God loves us enough to make us into the women we were created to be.

And stand with others whom we didn't study in the pages of this book. With Deborah who judged Israel; with Jael, the heroine who killed Sisera with a tent peg and freed Israel from his terror. Stand with Anna, the prophetess, one of the first to recognize Jesus as the redemption of Israel; and with Priscilla, who took the good news to the Gentiles. Stand with Junia the deaconess, a leader in the days of the apostles; and with Lydia and the church in her home. And stand with Mary, Jesus's mother, who believed the words of an angel that she would conceive, and then knelt at the foot of a Roman cross as her son died for us all. Stand with every woman whom God has called to be his own and who have answered that call.

Stand and hear the words spoken to another woman more than two thousand years ago, "Take heart, daughter; your faith has made you well" (Matthew 9:22).

God calls you to bear witness to his work of redemption. To his hope, to his healing. He calls you to lift your chin and dare to be the woman he's created you to be. To be filled with purpose and love, to step into the place he's prepared for you, a place of witness and wonder, of boldness and beauty. You are more than a conqueror through him who loves you.

And so you can say #MeToo not just to announce suffering and oppression, but to make a confident and courageous declaration with the women who followed Jesus and changed the world. Say it with them, say it with me—*Me too!*

> Therefore, since we are surrounded by so great
> a cloud of witnesses, let us also lay aside every
> weight, and sin which clings so closely, and let

us run with endurance the race that is set before us, looking to Jesus, the founder and perfecter of our faith, who for the joy that was set before him endured the cross, despising the shame, and is seated at the right hand of the throne of God.

Hebrews 12:1–2

A FINAL WORD

Thank you for traveling with me through the stories of many bold and brave women throughout the Bible. This journey was not what I expected it to be when I first set foot on the path of exploring the stories of women who had suffered from all kinds of abuse, prejudice, and oppression.

I did not expect to find a God who so fiercely loves and redeems women, who, even from the moment of his pronouncement that "he shall rule over you," has worked to overturn the bitter consequences of sin. But perhaps I should have known. After all, he who went to the cross for us would do no less.

So today, I look at my five daughters. I watch them developing into the women of God that he created them to be. I pray for them with a confidence I had not known before.

Perhaps, just perhaps, their world will be filled with a little less violence, a little less prejudice, a lot less oppression and denigration. A different world, a better one, that reflects the heart of God for women.

The distress I expected when delving into the stories of abuse and betrayal of women in the Bible has vanished. Instead, I find an incredible hope, and amazing love, a breathtaking wonder. For you. For me. And for the daughters who come after us.

For you, I pray that in your healing from whatever you have suffered, or are suffering now, you too will discover this God who fiercely loves you and seeks to redeem every tear, every bruise, every hurt that has lodged within your soul.

And I pray that you will dare to turn toward the One who loves you, who has always loved you, and be brave enough to believe in the love that invites you to live every day in the hope, the wonder, and the power of Christ's resurrection.

Me too,

Marlo

NOTES

Chapter 2. Sarai: Betrayed

1. Gordon Wenham, *Genesis 16–50*, Word Biblical Commentary, vol. 2, gen. eds. David A. Hubbard and Glenn W. Barker (Dallas: Word Books, 1994), 29–30.

Chapter 6. Hannah: Devalued

1. Beth Moore (@BethMooreLPM). Twitter, March 4, 2019, https://twitter.com/bethmoorelpm/status/11025767051248 72193?lang=en.

2. Kelly Ladd Bishop, "Captain Marvel and Woman Warriors," *Jesus Creed*, March 14, 2019, patheos.com, https://www.patheos.com/blogs/jesuscreed/2019/03/14/captain-marvel-and-woman-warriors/.

Chapter 8. Bathsheba: Sexualized

1. Catherine McCall, "The Sexualization of Women and Girls," *Psychology Today*, March 4, 2012, psychologytoday.com, https://www.psychologytoday.com/us/blog/overcoming-child-abuse/201203/the-sexualization-women-and-girls.

2. Jodi Kantor and Megan Twohey, "Sexual Misconduct Claims Trail a Hollywood Mogul," *The New York Times*, October 5, 2017, nytimes.com, https://www.nytimes.com/2017/10/05/us/harvey-weinstein-harassment-allegations.html.

3. Audrey Carlsen, Maya Salam, Claire Cain Miller, Denise Lu, Ash Ngu, Jugal K. Patel, Zach Wichter, "#MeToo Brought Down 201 Powerful Men. Nearly Half of Their Replacements Are Women," *The New York Times*, October 29, 2018, nytimes.com, https://www.nytimes.com/interactive/2018/10/23/us/metoo-replacements.html.

4. David Guzik, "2 Samuel 11—David's Adultery and Murder" commentary, accessed January 10, 2020, https://enduringword.com/bible-commentary/2-samuel-11/. Italics in the original.

Chapter 10. Mary and Martha: Oppressed

1. Meredith Fuller, "Why Are Some Women Nasty to Other Women," *Psychology Today*, August 4, 2013, psychologytoday.com.

2. Eliezer ben Hercanus (R. Eliezer), quoted in *The Mishnah*, Sotah 3.4 (New York: Oxford University Press, 1933), 296.

3. Michael Card, *Luke: The Gospel of Amazement*, Biblical Imagination Series (Downers Grove, IL: InterVarsity Press, 2011), 141.

4. John Cassian, quoted in *Ancient Christian Commentary on Scripture, New Testament III, Luke*, Arthur A. Just Jr., ed., (Downers Grove, IL: InterVarsity Press, 2003), 183.

Chapter 11. A Samaritan Woman: Shamed

Note: Portions of this chapter are loosely adapted from chapter 2 of my book, *Reaching for Wonder: Encountering Christ When Life Hurts* (Nashville: Abingdon, 2018), "Reaching through Shame: You've Had Five Husbands."

1. Quoted by Bruce Milne, *The Message of John*, The Bible Speaks Today, John R. W. Stott, ed. (Leicester, England: InterVarsity Press, 1993), 83.

2. Michael Card, *John: The Gospel of Wisdom*, Biblical Imagination Series (Downers Grove, IL: InterVarsity Press, 2014), 69.

3. Michael Card, *The Parable of Joy: Reflections on the Wisdom of the Book of John* (Nashville, TN: Thomas Nelson, 1995), 57.

Chapter 12. A Sinful Woman: Scorned

1. David E. Garland, *Luke*, Zondervan Exegetical Commentary on the New Testament, Clinton E. Arnold, gen. ed. (Grand Rapids, MI: Zondervan, 2011), 325.

Chapter 13. A Woman Caught in Adultery: Blamed

Note: Portions of this chapter are loosely adapted from chapter 12 of my book, *Reaching for Wonder: Encountering Christ When Life Hurts* (Nashville: Abingdon, 2018), "Reaching through Guilt: The First Stone."

1. Bede, quoted in *John 1–10,* Ancient Christian Commentary on Scripture, New Testament Iva, Joel C. Elowsky, ed., Thomas C. Oden, gen. ed. (Downers Grove, IL: IVP Academic, 2014), 274.

Chapter 14. Women at the Tomb: Witnesses to Wonder

1. Josephus, *Antiquities of the Jews,* 4.8.15.

ABOUT THE AUTHOR

As a young adult Marlo Schalesky prayed fervently that God would give her the gift of healing, not of bodies but of hearts. She had no idea what that meant. These days, she's starting to get a clue. Today, what she loves most is finding and revealing the wonder of God in those places in life where we least expect it—in the hurts and hardships, in the moments that go awry, in random flowers that poke up through pavement, in a child's first touch of a horse's silky coat.

Marlo is a horse-girl through and through. When she was a child, she played horses on the playground, drew very poor pictures of ponies (now she sticks to writing), and ferreted away dimes, quarters, and birthday money in hopes of owning her first horse someday. At nine years old, that dream came true when she bought her first little chestnut gelding, Hustling Hobo. She escaped the painful parts of childhood by riding him through the woods, up and down hills, and under trees, the two of them fellow adventurers in the wild world, running free and happy. She believes those early experiences planted the seeds of what would become her adult ministry of using horses to bring hope and healing to gang-impacted, foster, homeless, and other kids who need the wonder of horses in their lives as much as she did. Today, she's putting her master's degree in theology to work as the executive director of Wonder Wood Ranch, the charity she founded on her and her husband's property.

Most of her days are now spent partnering with her own six children (all horse-lovers themselves) to introduce the healing power of animals into the lives of kids who have experienced horrific trauma, and young women who have already been broken by more #MeToo moments than can even be imagined. Every day, as she and her family work with these young people, her heart is broken. And then it's healed again as she witnesses the power of God at work through horses and donkeys, piggies and goats, bunnies and chinchillas, guinea pigs, chickens, giant oak trees, and quiet paths on horseback. She has seen over and over that healing doesn't come through a person but rather through simply listening without judgment, without condemnation, and by making a space for God to work his miracles of wonder in broken hearts and souls.

If you'd like to know more about Marlo or her other books, visit her website at VividGod.com. You can also find her thoughts on discovering the wonder of God in everyday life on Facebook (facebook.com/MarloSchalesky) or Twitter (twitter.com/MarloSchalesky). If you're a horse-girl too (or wish you were), check out Wonder Wood Ranch at WonderWoodRanch.org and follow the Ranch on Facebook (facebook.com/WonderWoodRanch) or Instagram.